TEIDA'S STORY

TEIDA'S STORY

LIFE THROUGH THE EYES OF A DOG

Danielle Corrie

CONTENTS

Dedicated to our friend George
who has now passed away

A NEW DAY, A NEW BEGINNING

Today is a glorious spring morning. Beams of light dapple the tiny insects scurrying in the dew. Flowers nod their sleepy heads. Flashes of sun peep through the garden to climb into a blue sky. *Why do I have the feeling that today, for some reason, is not going to be a normal day?*

Linda, my owner, is holding the cordless phone, her nimble fingers dialling. 'I hope someone answers … Damn! I'll try their mobile,' I hear Linda say. She is drumming her fingers against the wall. She paces up and down the back pathway. Sweat pours off of her. I sense that she is anxious.

She starts talking; her voice is high and clipped. The finger drumming continues.

'Oh, thank you!' A sudden relief is in her voice. She leans against the wall, a great breath coming out of her. 'Teida and I will be there in an hour.' *Was that my name I just heard? Who is she talking to? How am I part of this conversation?*

I follow Linda into the laundry room as she hangs up the phone. Grabbing my blue lead from a rusty hook over the rattling washing machine, she gets me ready to go for a mid-morning stroll. Just the two of us. It isn't often that Linda and I are able to hang out on our own. I bark, excited, as she bends to put the leash round my neck. She smiles, but there is a hurt behind her eyes. Part of me is happy as I wonder where our walk will take us today, but something is wrong. We're heading towards the car, but it's not in the usual place. I follow Linda.

As soon as the car door opens, I leap up onto my seat, right next to Linda. We drive away, our cozy home receding into the distance. This time, Linda decides to drive in a different direction to our normal routine. Instead of turning left, we turn right. Instead of driving up a very steep hill, we are on a flatter yet bumpier road passing a shopping center I have never seen before. There are other cars on the left and right of us. Swerving around a corner, I nearly fall over.

—*Slow down Linda. Why are you driving this way?*

I look at Linda. With a sheer determined look on her face, she is definitely on a mission. Something just doesn't seem right.

Not a word is spoken. There is no music playing on the car stereo, not even Linda's favourite music that she always plays to cheer herself up when she is down. The silence is deafening. So I decide to bark. I then lift my paws and place them gently on Linda's lap. She pushes them away. I lick her hand. I even nuzzle her with my nose. 'Not now Teida … '

Tension fills the air. *What do I do? Why is Linda treating me this way? What's wrong?* Linda knows she can talk to me. She has been my owner ever since I can remember. She's my family.

I remember the day Linda came to collect me. I was the last pup left. My mama was nuzzling me and I was hiding my head against her body. I finally peered upwards and noticed that Linda was not like the angry man who came beforehand. Her eyes gave me hope. They were soft, like my mama's warm fur. Linda came forward and picked me up, patting my mama at the same time, telling her not to worry, she would take good care of me. I remember a feeling of weightlessness as she lifted me into the palm of her hand, caressing my body so tenderly. Linda carefully put me in a small box and we drove away. My new home waited.

Today, things are different. *What's wrong? Is it me?*

I smell my food, toys, bedding, leash, and that annoying medication. It's all in here with us. Everything neatly placed on the back seat. *Where are we going? Are we moving again?* Linda and I have moved house many times and been to many places, but that can't be what's happening now, can it?

I usually like going out with Linda but with this total silence and being ignored, perhaps it would have been better if I was left at home. Linda is acting so differently to normal.

Our journey ends. We are now in front of an unfamiliar place, a house I have never seen before. Following behind Linda, I pass a white car that is larger than usual and has strange markings down the side. Squeezing between the car and the fence, I discover garden beds surrounding me from all angles. The scent of the gardens fills my nose. We pass through a side gate leading through to a back deck with many pot plants displayed in rows against the back window, being shaded from the hot sun. Two unfamiliar people, a man and a woman, are at a table. They stand. Looking up from where I am, their heads appear to almost touch the roof. The lady appears to be quiet and a bit nervous. She has soft looking brown hair cascading down her back. She gently puts the back of her hand towards my face, allowing me to sniff her. The man stands silently before me. They introduce themselves as Annie and George.

Peaceful, serene energy surrounds this environment. Maybe Linda and I are moving here? As Linda talks with Annie and George, I quietly make my way into the garden. I am alone in a new world of smells, sounds, and sights, surrounded by many shadows.

The wind picks up. Chimes and bells hanging from above sound their chorus in the breeze. A loud slam interrupts my exploration. *What was that?* The side gate has locked itself. Returning to the back deck, in front of me is a round red bucket filled with water. It smells fresh. I lap it up. The cool water feels good on my tongue. At the same time, Linda's car starts up and pulls away.

She's left without saying goodbye. *Where is she going? Will I see her again? Why is she leaving me here?* Annie and George do not say anything. There is no need. I can tell that they know what is going on. Perhaps Annie was the person Linda spoke to earlier.

Fences surround me on every side, too high to jump. From this very moment, my instincts tell me that after six years with Linda, this place is my new home. I will miss her, but I can already tell that this is a wonderful place to be.

My attention is drawn to the aroma of the sweet-smelling flowers. The scents of lemon, passionfruit, and lavender fill the air as I explore my new backyard. I am enveloped by the scent of summer roses and by fields of yellow and white daisies. In the far corner, a tall blue and orange flower reaches up to the sun. Soft pink and white petals have fallen onto the grass below. They feel good beneath my paws. A stone and pebble pathway leads to another large side gate. It looks shiny. The gate smells like new paint. It's clear that someone devotes a lot of time to this garden. There is no trace of another dog. No scents, sounds or sights tell me that another is here. What an opportunity! I set about marking my territory with great pride.

Peeping through the pale wooden fence, I see that this house is on a street corner. Instead of another yard, I see beds of grass meeting it on the other side. There are dogs on leashes, people strolling, children playing. The sounds of my new world fill my ears. Occasionally, cars drive past, slowly, their engines humming. A man in a cap shields his forehead from the sun.

Annie and George go inside and I follow them. In front of me I see light colored woollen carpet and blue toned rugs spread far and wide, along the walls and underneath the chairs, lounges and tables. Paintings, photos and memorabilia hang on the walls, displaying compassion and welcoming love. The vapours of an oil burner fill my nostrils. I sniff at everything I pass. In the dining room, I notice a small wooden box with many tiny bottles of scented oils leaning against the legs of a wooden table. Sitting on her sofa, Annie puts her feet up and George sits next to her drinking a strong-smelling cup of coffee. I sit nearby, observing, yet keeping my distance at the same time.

After a short time, George rises, finishes his coffee and says his goodbyes. I hear the front door close, followed by the sound of an engine close by, receding into the distance. Now I know who the white car with the strange markings belongs to. *Where is he going? I thought George lives here too?*

'Welcome Teida. I hope you enjoy living here with me and adjusting to your new home. It's the first time I've had a dog stay with me. Come on.' Annie stands up, gesturing for me to follow.

She leads me from room to room, her hand occasionally ruffling my ears.

'Make yourself at home Teida,' she says absently, her hand at the nape of my neck. It feels good. 'Tell me if you need to go outside to the toilet if I do not take you out in time.'

Night time arrives. After a long day full of confusion and change, I am tired. Annie takes me to a smaller room, located opposite the kitchen, near the back door. I find my bedding ready on the floor waiting for me. 'Teida, this is your bedroom. Good night. I'll see you in the morning.' Annie closes the door behind me. I sit and wait a while. Soft footsteps follow, and soon the house is enveloped in darkness. My eyes grow heavy.

The place smells like where Linda washed her clothes – a laundry room. A washing machine sits in the corner, with a sink beside it. This room is all for me. I settle down into my bedding, and between my exhaustion after the day's excursion, and the soothing sounds of the night time chorus coming through the window, it's not long before I curl up, wrap my tail around my body, and go to sleep.

Dawn rises, and a ray of sunlight touches my face. It's warm. The door opens and I wag my tail in greeting as I rise from the bedding. 'Morning Teida,' Annie says, a smile on her face and a mug of fruit juice in her hand. 'Did you sleep well last night?' Stretching, I realize I have been away from Linda for a whole day and night. Blinking and yawning, I watch Annie fill up my food bowl. The same dry food kibble Linda used to give me. *What will today bring?*

I enjoy my freedom as Annie and I both go outside, the backyard greeting my nose with fresh morning air. A new day and a new beginning. No more chaos. No more fighting for food or attention. No more trying to fit in or defend myself. One on one company with a lady living on her own, willing to share her home and devote her time to take care of me. Annie's eyes, as bright as the flowers around her, reflect the essence of love and understanding.

I love her. From that moment, she is my Mother.

After a run outside in the garden my curiosity is sated and we return to the lounge room. I find a new spot in the corner in between two large sofas where I nestle myself. Mother sits nearby on the sofa, reading. The front door is left open, allowing the cool fresh breeze to find its way inside. I'm interrupted by an unfamiliar noise. Someone is outside, coming towards the front door. Their footsteps are heavy, but somehow sound familiar. It could be Linda! My tail begins to shake in anticipation. The wire screen door opens. Walking towards the front door, I see George. He is holding something rolled up in his hand. What can it be? It is probably something for Mother.

'Hello Annie. Hello Teida! How did you survive last night? Here, I have something for you. It's a welcome present. Come and have a look,' George says as he makes his way inside. 'Come on!' *What, a welcome present for me? How kind and thoughtful George is!*

George unrolls the present onto the floor, and it spreads out, covering the whole area between the two lounges. Something tough that I can't pull apart with my claws. I sniff and put my paws upon this blanket-like object, before sinking myself in further, feeling the soft padded foam beneath me and the rope-like hessian keeping me snug and warm. *Now I have made another friend; a big brother or fatherly figure.* With both Mother and George's affection comes a sense of belonging, as if I have been here my whole life. With this feeling there is nowhere else I would rather be. *I have a place I can call home.*

Mother and George sit on the couch together. Looking in their direction and watching them, their loyalty and friendship shines like a beacon. They talk, and as I listen, I learn they are volunteers for an emergency service organisation. They speak in hushed whispers as they prepare for an important meeting. There is a lot of organisation of people and schedules involved in this upcoming event.

MOTHER OFF TO WORK

Following Mother around the house early in the morning, I am curious to know what is happening. First she is in the bathroom, and I hear the sound of rushing water through the door; then the bedroom, and a rustle of clothes as I wait outside; and finally, the kitchen, where the smell of food reaches my nose. I sit nearby. *Mother is getting ready for work. I wonder how long it will be before she goes?*

'Teida, come here. Now I need you to listen to me carefully. I am going off to work now. You need to go outside in the backyard. While I am at work I need you to be a good girl and mind the house until I come home. On the deck there is water in your red bucket for you to drink and food in your bowl so you have something to eat. By the time I come home it will be starting to get dark.'

Not moving a muscle, attentively staring into Mother's eyes as she crouches down to my level, I soon become aware of what is being communicated to me. Even though it may not seem to you humans that we understand, dogs are able to tune in and sense exactly what is going on.

Even deeper, there are times where I feel almost human. My physical appearance is a dog and I express myself from a dog's perspective: barking, running around and not having a care in the world. Deep inside, though, I know I am different. Inside I feel both dog and human, recognizing energies and feelings of those around me. I can tell what makes someone happy and what makes someone sad, what makes their mind tick and what they are thinking at this very moment. I can see – no, *feel* – their soul. *Do I have a soul?*

Intuitively tuning to understand Mother's mind is something I am coming to terms with being in this new environment. Connecting, bonding and understanding how she really feels and what she really longs for deep, deep inside. When I first arrived, I knew that even though Mother appeared nervous and uncertain on the outside, on the inside she was looking forward to having me as part of her life. I can tell from the way she looks at me that she's been looking forward to having a dog in her life for a long, long while.

We walk together to the back door. Mother opens the door. I walk outside, my claws pattering against the paving slabs. 'Bye Teida, see you when I get home.' The back door closes before Mother leaves and the front door clatters shut behind her. It's time to explore my new surroundings.

Stepping on the soft lawn, which sparkles and shines, still wet from the morning dew, I come across my toys. They smell different to when they were at Linda's. *Where are these new smells coming from?* The world is silent around me. Not a sound; no movements. The cold morning air swirls around the garden. I look up, watching the fluffy white clouds create a variety of shapes as they join together then break apart. An object in the distance roars as it crawls across the sky.

All of a sudden I hear rumbling in the distance. Is it thunder, telling me a storm is nearby? I realize that it's the sound of a train passing. I didn't know Mother lived near a train station.

Peeping through the fence palings I see well dressed people walking, their strides long and powerful, their shoes clunking as they make their way to their destination. Maybe, like Mother, these people need to get a train to work too. I bark. Not a loud bark, just one to say hello.

They walk straight past. *Did anyone even notice me?* All these people seem to be in a world of their own. With the sun now beaming down, I go and have a drink from my bucket. Astonishment and surprise! All my dry kibble food is poured all over the floor! There are many birds nearby, hanging around chuckling to each other; playing a practical joke. *Who invited them?* Like a rocket, I scamper towards them and make them flurry into the air.

Strange noises now come from the front yard. *Where is it coming from? Our driveway or next door?* With my ears pinned to the back door, I listen. Oh no! Someone is inside! *Who is it? Has Mother come home early?* The squeaky back door creaks open as I stay on the other side, totally alert until I see who it is. What an unexpected surprise: it's George!

—*Hi George, what are you doing here?* I ask, wagging my tail in excitement. *Don't you go to work like Mother does?*

As George places his belongings on the outdoor table, I place one of my toys at his feet.

—*George, do you want to play with me?* I sit in anticipation, waiting for his reaction.

Eventually, George picks up the toy in his large, worn out hands. He throws it way across the yard. With a huge grin from ear to ear, I run straight after it. Jumping and leaping into the air, the toy lands in my mouth without touching the ground. *What a catch!*

As the sun continues to rise, the heat gets to me. I start puffing and panting. George ambles back to sit under the shade of the deck for a while, before going inside then coming out again with a mug of hot coffee in one hand and a biscuit in the other. He plonks himself onto one of the wooden slat chairs. I notice he is gasping for air too and sweating in the shade. George appears to have gone through a lot in his life. I cannot put my paw on it, but something just isn't right. Munching into a biscuit and sipping his cup of coffee, George makes some phone calls. I take a drink from my water bowl and stay close by.

'Teida, how are you adjusting to living with Annie? I know yesterday was hard for you to deal with. I want to let you know that Annie needs you. From what I saw yesterday, you will fit in easily to her lifestyle. She has never had a dog before. You are her first. I can already see a bond forming between the two of you. Annie needs someone to watch over her. Four days ago she came home from work to find her home broken into. Teida, you have a very important job here – to watch over Annie and keep guard over her home. Do you think you can do that?'

I look up into George's eyes and thump my tail on the ground.

—*Of course I can George.*

George gives me a pat and continues. 'Annie wakes up really early. She works long hours Teida. Annie sometimes leaves for work very early and comes home after dark. You will be out in the backyard for a long time until she's home and Annie will be very tired when she gets home at night.'

George sips more of his coffee.

'I don't live here, but I pop in and out when I can. You see Teida, I have my own family. Annie means the world to me. We have a very special friendship and I am only a phone call away if she needs anything. I know you and I will become great mates too.'

George finishes his cup of coffee and rises from the wooden deck chair. 'I have to go now. I will leave everything in your capable paws.' He waves goodbye and goes.

With George now gone, I find some shade under the tree in Mother's garden and reflect on everything George has just told me. *How terrible for Mother to have her home broken into. Now Mother has me, there is no way that is ever going to happen again. I'm glad that George isn't too far away when Mother needs someone. I like him. I hope that George and I can become good friends too.*

A sound of rustling interrupts my thoughts. Landing on the grass near the clothes line, the birds return. This time I am prepared. *You are not going to get near my food this time!* I start bounding towards them, my tongue flapping in the wind and a bark on my lips. The birds fly onto the roof and the telegraph pole nearby and at the same time, I run into a sticky thread hanging down in front of me. A big, brown spider trembles on the thread, its back as big as a walnut. It climbs further upwards, balancing without falling.

—*Hello, I'm Mrs Spider. Sorry my web is in your way.*

—*My name is Teida. I am chasing the birds who have been trying to eat my dinner. Your web is so nearly invisible that I didn't see it.*

—*Thank you Teida. Did you know we use our webs to trap our food; insects that pass by like flies or mosquitoes?*

—*No I didn't, Mrs Spider. You are very clever.*

—*Teida, I see you are new here and you play a lot in the garden amongst the plants and shrubs. I want to warn you to be careful of the thorns on the outside of some of the plants. They are very spiky, and they can hurt. With your delicate paws Teida, I do not want you treading on one.*

—*Thank you Mrs Spider. I will watch out and be careful.*

Now with the birds up high, I roll on the grass back and forth, feeling the dryness of the ground beneath me. It has not rained for a while.

Shaking off the grass, I amble through the garden. I come across a lemon tree, the same lemon tree I saw when I first arrived. Now, with the sun beaming down, the leaves have created protection from the sun, keeping the earth underneath nice and cool. I settle here for a while, crossing my paws over one another. Looking around, and remembering what Mrs

Spider told me, I notice the roses with their prickly thorns taking in the heat of the day. Alongside them is a large palm tree, with prickly fronds hanging from its branches. *Imagine treading on a thorn or prickly palm frond. Ouch!* That would hurt my paw.

MILLIE

My insight tells me someone else lives within Annie's garden, like a fairy or leprechaun hiding from the human world. *I wonder who it is?* Animals have a sixth sense. We can detect and communicate with a loved one in spirit, whether it is a deceased animal or a person. Walking further, deep within the lush green canopy filtering in the bright sunlight, I discover a small-statured elderly lady bent over and tending to Mother's roses. Taking a step back into the shade, I see her holding a pair of secateurs in one hand and a watering can in the other. She is wearing thick eye glasses that are sitting on the top of her nose. Her curly hair, turned silver-gray by age, is neatly pushed away from her face. Holding a wooden cane, the lady hobbles towards me, introducing herself.

—*Hello Teida, welcome to your new home. My name is Millie.*

I crouch low and take a step back. *How does she know my name?*

—*There is no need to be afraid.* Millie reassures me. *I am Annie's grandma, and like all the fairies and leprechauns, I live in Annie's garden. Being a gardener all my life, I help Annie with her plants, making them grow happy and healthy. I sit and have a chat to Annie's garden each day, and make sure that each plant big or small has enough sunlight, nutrients and water to grow and blossom.*

—Millie, how do you know how to best take care of each plant? I ask, curious.

—*Well, when I water the plants I give them enough to drink without letting them drown. Some need a drizzle, others need a shower. Plants tell me by standing tall and strong, their leaves upright and not droopy and they sparkle in the sunlight.*

The nutrients are in the soil. Some soils are gluggy and clay-like where the plant roots find it difficult to spread out and it looks like they never grow at all. Other soils are sandy, where the water drains freely. Many plants like this condition. Mother's soil is perfect for all the plants in her garden.

Seeing that I am interested in Mother's garden and flowers, Millie continues.

—*Did you know that a garden teaches one the lesson of patience? Not all plants grow at the same speed. A flower on a delicate magnolia flowers only once a year. Being so fragile, they can be blown away by a gust of wind. Meanwhile, the fruits of lemon and mandarin trees can take a few months before they ripen and are ready to eat. Annie's geraniums and daisies flower throughout the year, while her annuals totally disappear and then reappear like all of Annie's spring and summer flowering bulbs.*

As one plant finishes flowering, another starts to blossom. There are flowers in Annie's garden all throughout the year. Some of Annie's plants, instead of flowers, have beautiful leaves of different colors.

—*Do you have a favourite flower, Millie?*

—*Roses are my favourite flower. Roses represent to me the beauty of the spirit realm – showing who we really are. I can just sit with a rose, absorb its scent, and feel a stillness and presence. Roses allow me to be in tune with my whole self. They bring their fragrance from the spirit world to the earth world.*

Millie pauses for a moment, looking lost in her memories.

—*Teida, when I was alive, I grew many different roses in my garden. There was such an assortment of colors. Tones of blue, red, pink, white, yellow, and orange, spread far and wide, all displaying large beautiful blooms. My roses were as big as dinner plates. I won many rose competitions Teida, because they were so beautiful.*

—*Millie, you must have had so many roses in your garden. Do you have one that is special to you?'*

—*Well Teida, all my roses were special to me. I liked the old standard rose varieties as well the latest hybrid rose species. Each rose had its own individual characteristic and smell. I used to be able to tell a rose by its scent. Some of the rose species I had dated back to the 1800s, and in that time they used those varieties in the making of French perfume. Even today, roses are used to make essential oils like rosehip, rosewood and rose otto, or just pure rose oil.*

I remember the smell of the scented oils burning yesterday, and the small wooden box on the floor containing tiny bottles of essential oils. *I wonder if Mother has any of the rose oils Millie just mentioned?*

Captivated by Millie's words of experience and wisdom, I give my nose a work out, discovering the many new fragrances and smells of these beautiful roses. Some roses in Mother's garden are standing tall, close to the brick wall at the back. Others have thin stems and are planted to the right of the lemon tree. As I look left towards the fence leading onto the street, I notice even more roses, protected by the shade of the mandarin tree. There are roses with refreshing, soothing smells, sweet yet subtle. Then there are others that have a stronger odour, sharp and uplifting. Some of Mother's roses have no smell at all. They are not in bloom. Instead, as I look up, I see tiny rose buds forming at the tops of their long stems, growing up towards the sun; whilst others have new leaves and stems forming. All of Mother's roses are in different stages of growth.

Feeling something soft and silky between my paws, I look down. In front of me are rose petals of different colors. Red, pink, white, and even purple. The wind last night must have blown some of the flowers off. Walking along the front of Mother's rose garden, I see miniature roses, not even as tall as me, with delicate pale pink flowers that sway in the breeze. Besides roses, I come across blue and white, bell-like flowers, delicate and soft, with dome shaped petals drooping to the ground. These flowers are just the right size for garden fairies to make their home. In contrast, next to them are large red, orange and white toned flowers with strapping green leaves. There is so much beauty surrounding me, from the moist earth underneath my paws to the sap of the trees and shrubs, even the wooden logs and bricks bordering each of the garden beds are neat and pretty.

Looking around, I see Millie coming out into the open, holding a cup of tea. She walks towards the edge of the garden bed, pondering over the neatly manicured roses, and stops near the lemon tree. She pauses and takes a sip of her tea. I wander over to her. It appears Millie wants to tell me more.

—*Teida, do you want to know the story of how Annie came to live here?*

—*Please tell me, Millie.* I sprawl across the straw-like mulch spread under the shade of Mother's lemon tree. With Mother still at work, and George telling me not to expect her home until after dark, I had wondered how to pass the time until she came home. Now Millie is here to keep my company and satisfy my curiosity.

Millie sits down on one of the rocks under the tree, takes another sip of her tea and starts talking.

—*Teida, when Annie was looking for a home, I was there. Annie always wanted a home with a garden. Not just any garden. Her dream was to have a home with a large garden, where the front door was away from the front gate. Like her mother and me, Annie loves gardening. Since Annie didn't have her own car, she also needed a home within walking distance to the shops and public transport to travel to and from work. Inside her previous homes, she always enjoyed soaking in a deep big bath tub.*

Finally, with George's help, searching high and low for the perfect house to make her home, they came across this one. Shops located at the end of the street; a train station nearby; a quiet, friendly neighbourhood; and George only a short distance away by car. Inside was a great big bath and outside was potential garden space where Annie could imagine creating her own garden both out the front and out the back. This place was perfect in every way. The following weekend Annie took her parents and sister and showed them this house, the house she longed to make her new home. The very same day Annie went outside to the backyard with her sister.

Can you guess what happened then, Teida?

—No, Millie – tell me.'

Millie takes a breath and continues.

—Sitting on the edge of the back deck, Annie and her sister both looked ahead. Right in front of them they saw a raised, bare, desolate garden bed with only the stump of a large tree in the center and a pot plant to the side, trying to hide a large brick wall. All of a sudden, an unexpected vision appeared before both of them. An image of a person they both knew. A lady who lived on this earth and now has passed away. Teida, the vision Annie and her sister saw was me. My face in the middle of this same, dry, empty garden bed; with only clumps of plants squashed way up in the back corner next to the old wooden paling fence. I had a mission Teida. I needed to deliver Annie a very important message. This house was to be her new home. She had to buy this property and create a rose garden. With the support of her family and George, that is exactly what Annie did.

Listening to Millie, I now understand Mother's connection to her garden and the reason behind her decision to make this place her beautiful home.

—Teida, before I go, there is something else you may not know. Annie's sister is someone you have seen before. You will realize this when you both meet.

Enjoy every moment in your new home Teida. Enjoy being with Annie. She needs you.

I have learnt a lot about my new home and about Mother, and now I have a new question to think about. Millie told me I know Annie's sister. *Who is she? How could I have met her before?*

WHO ELSE DO I MEET?

I wander down the side of my new home where a neighbouring fence meets mine. An area I have yet to explore. Peering through the fence, another dog stares back from the other side, investigating his new neighbour. Inquisitive, and much bigger than me, with a black and gray coat, prominent eyebrows and a gray moustache, he sniffs the air as he looks at me.

—*Hello, who are you?* he asks.

—*I'm Teida. I just moved in.*

He looks happy and starts filling me in on important dog information about the area.

—*Welcome Teida. My name is Austin. I've been here my whole life. There are cats living in the house behind me and the neighbour next door has a cat. It is the first time I have had a dog as a next door neighbour. How old are you? I'm six. It is very nice to meet you. I have to go now. I can hear my family returning. Chat soon.*

How nice it is to have a dog friend the same age as me! How lonely Austin must have been before! From this moment, each day, when Mother and Austin's family leave for work, Austin and I start chatting, discussing the world from a dog's point of view.

Yes, like humans, dogs talk too. We talk in our own language only dogs can understand. In the animal world, I can find out who the new pet in the street is, who is leaving, and what other critters come and visit, which is particularly useful if things happen at night time or when I am inside. In the human world, I discover who is dating who, who has moved into or out of the neighbourhood, and become familiar with the new noises – renovations, new cars, even the large trucks that come our way. If only humans and dogs talk the same language! Imagine what I am able to tell Mother!

Even though they don't understand, I still contribute to human conversations in my own dog ways, using my tail and voice and ears and lots of other signals so that the humans around me can have a clue as to how I am feeling and what I think about the things I hear and see. I believe they get the general idea about what I am saying. But the neighbourhood dogs definitely know; we inform each other who is boss, particularly when it comes to our territories, our homes.

There is more barking from homes close by. We say hello to one another, and find out what has been happening in each other's world. When one dog starts, I cannot resist the temptation to join in and have a chat. I soon become familiar with which bark belongs to which dog. We also bark to say to be careful, and have another bark to deter unwanted animals from our home. We tell the cats to stay away. Unlike us dogs, many neighbourhood cats tend to wander away from their homes. I wonder if their owners are ever on the lookout for them?

Returning to the back deck after talking to Austin, I walk along the wooden fence palings lying on the ground. I take a step up onto the side deck near the back shed then another step down onto the concrete pathway below between the two garden beds. Just as I get near my destination I am stopped suddenly in my tracks.

—*Look out!*

Looking around I am unable to see anything.

—*Down here. You nearly trod on me.*

—*Oh, I'm sorry!* I see a minute black spot on the ground in front of me staring back. A tiny insect is in between the crevices, camouflaging itself as it crawls along the gray concrete footpath. *Who are you?*

—*I'm Mr Ant. I live in the dirt, well protected amongst the grass. Can you imagine what it is like to be very tiny? No bigger than a speck on the ground, surrounded by grass as thick and as dense as a forest, flowers as tall as a tree. We hide anywhere. Under a leaf, under rocks and stones or even a flower pot, keeping ourselves safe from predators. I am out on my daily walk, cleaning up any food scraps. You're new here, right?*

—*My name is Teida! I have recently moved in. I am out here keeping guard whilst my owner Annie is at work.*

—*Nice to meet you Teida. Perhaps I can introduce you to Mr Worm and some of the lizard families who live nearby.*

As we travel back along the garden path to the middle of the lawn, a slimy looking head appears.

—*Hello Mr Ant.*

—*Hello Mr Worm! I want to introduce you to a new resident, Teida, who has just moved in. You have probably seen her chasing those birds who hang around the back yard.*

—*Hello Teida, I'm Mr Worm. I keep the soil soft and pliable, giving it nutrients that make it healthy so all of the plants in the garden can grow. I have to thank you for keeping the birds at bay so early in the morning, otherwise they pull us worms up through the dirt with their beaks and have one or two for dinner. Have you heard of the saying the early bird catches the worm?*

—*I have, Mr Worm, and thanks for your explanation. I now understand what it means.*

—*Have you met any of the lizards Teida? The birds also eat lizards and there are many lizard families living in the garden beds. They look similar in shape to us worms. One difference between the lizards and us earthworms is lizards have patterns on their skin and aren't so slimy. The lizards come in all different sizes and they mainly hide under the house or near rocks, but they love to come out and bask in the sun. Be careful where you walk, as they have a tendency to camouflage themselves. There is no need to be afraid of them though. They are harmless.*

—*It's nice to meet you Teida*, said Mr Ant.

—*We're glad you're here Teida*, Mr Worm agreed.

After meeting Millie and all my new animal friends I walk back along the concrete pathway dividing the lawn from Mother's garden beds. I settle down to have a rest under a burgundy shrub that shades me from the sun. I suddenly collide with a small rock. The rock starts moving, with eyes that peer before me. However, rocks don't move. *Perhaps it isn't a rock after all?*

—Hello? I ask. *I'm Teida, is someone in there?*

I sniff and prod at the rock until a spongy looking head appears from within.

—*Hello, I'm Sally Snail. Do you know what you bumped into isn't a rock? It is my protective outer coating, my shell. It fits me like a glove from all sides, covering my body so that I can hide from predators. For me to come out and munch on a delicious leaf is quite a risk! Like many challenges and opportunities in life, Teida, you have to take a risk and stick your neck out. And when you do, it is very rewarding.*

Slithering away, Sally Snail disappears into the wilderness. I am left with words of wisdom from what I thought was a small rock in the garden.

Digging about, sinking lower, and carefully ensuring none of Mother's plants are damaged in the process, I create a nest for myself. After such a busy morning, finally I settle in for my afternoon nap.

ALL IN AN AFTERNOON

Boys and girls of different ages walk past the fence, wearing uniforms with the shirts hanging out and crinkled tunics. School must be finished. They must be going home. Not long after, dogs on leashes pass by. Barking loudly with my ears pointing to the sky, I rush towards the side fence once again.

Approaching the fence, brushing past yellow bushes in full flower, I hear a buzzing sound, closer and closer, louder and louder. Bees dive in and out of the flowers, searching for nectar and pollen. They're having fun; bouncing from one flower to another before they fly away.

A black spotted dog comes towards the fence and pauses.

—*Hello,* I bark from the other side. Before he has time to answer, his owner yanks the leash and pulls him away. Maybe she thinks I'll bite, but all I am doing is introducing myself.

Running back and forth along the grass a number of times during the day, my creative talents set in. Landscaping a distinctive pathway, winding and curving along the front of the lawn. Very innovative, don't you think?

Being outside and knowing I have the responsibility of protecting my new home, I decide to invent games. One game of mine is hide-and-seek. Have you ever played hide-and-seek before? Well, this is hide-and-seek, dog style. I crawl underneath the house, amongst the wooden slats. It is as if I am playing doggie limbo. No one can see me here. I lie down, my head hidden deep within the sandy earth. Someone walks past the side fence, and I bolt out of my hiding place, running towards them and growling. I become covered in dirt from my nose right up to my eyes, changing the color of my muzzle area dusty brown.

Wandering back away from the fence now my duty is done, the strong scent of the mandarin tree captures my attention, as well as the aroma of the large lemon tree Millie and I were sitting under not so long ago. All this running and barking has reminded me of something that makes me sad, and I am thinking about it as I walk through the garden.

—*Ouch!* My paw hurts. *Is that a prickly thorn I just trod on? Mrs Spider only warned me a few hours ago to be careful of these!*

Despairingly, I slowly hobble back through the soft lawn onto the hard floor of the back deck. Rest time! I settle close to the back door, snoozing – my afternoon siesta. I keep my eyes half open, keeping watch. My ears point to the sky, alert for any unfamiliar sounds.

—*What have I done to my paw?* I start licking my paw in the hope it will heal before Mother comes home.

—Teida I notice you are licking your paw. Are you all right? comes a voice from above.

—Hello Mrs Spider, remember how you told me to be careful of those thorns? Mrs Spider nods. *Well, I think I just trod on one, and now my paw is throbbing. It hurts. I hope it gets better before Mother gets home. I don't want to cause trouble for her.*

I take a breath and continue.

—I became distracted, Mrs Spider. I have been thinking how my previous owner Linda and I parted ways.

—What happened Teida?

I start to tell her the story. I was just defending myself. I lived with Linda and another lady who had two dogs and children. These dogs were bigger but younger than me. They were totally disobedient, mischievous and seemed to get away with everything: from digging holes to pulling clothes off the line and even damaging shoes left outside the back door. They needed rules and boundaries. It frustrated me that they never were in trouble for anything. I was the always the one to blame.

So I took it upon myself to teach these dogs right from wrong – dog style. I could see what was wrong. Dogs teach dogs manners better than humans do. We speak the same language and know dog etiquette. Humans only know a few words here and there like 'sit', 'stay' and 'no', and they misinterpret our body language a lot of the time. I was always the aggressor, but in fact I was just trying to be dominant. These dogs never learned to respect their owner, whereas I really respected Linda. This particular day, I was snarling and growling, telling these dogs who was boss. We got into a big fight, where one of the younger dogs became injured. The children came outside, saw blood on the floor and then went running back inside crying. Linda came outside, and I saw the sadness in her eyes. I knew I had disappointed her. After being with Linda for nearly six years, it was time to part ways.

—*That is how I ended up here*, I finished.

By this time, all my new animal friends had gathered around, listening to my story, and offering their advice. Sally Snail, Mr Worm, Mr Ant and even Austin had come over to the fence.

—*Don't worry Teida. You just need to be yourself here. There are no dogs to discipline. Like Millie said, all you have to do is look after your new home and watch over Annie. You are good at that Teida. I have been watching you. Here is where you belong,* said Mr Worm.

—*People can be like that,* Austin explained further. *I live with a family of children and adults and believe me; they can be temperamental at times. They do not seem to understand things from a dog's point of view. Being the oldest, you always get the blame for everything. As long as humans treat you well, then you know you belong. If your owners change their mind about taking care of you, no matter what caused them to do so, it is better that you find a new place to live, a place you can call home.*

Austin continued with his words of wisdom.

—*There is no need to take things personally Teida. Humans tend to hide from their pets what is bothering them. It is up to us to find out what the real cause is and help them.*

I think about what Austin said, then share my thoughts.

—*Just before I came here, I heard Linda say to her friends and family how much she wants to have children of her own. Linda* said to them that she couldn't cope with another mishap like that and feared that I may be too possessive. So I guess the incidents with the dogs aren't the real cause after all.

—Now you're talking. So the whole thing wasn't your fault after all. It was your time to move on, and you will have just as much fun with Annie and George in your new home. There is no need to feel guilty, said Austin.

The evening sun will soon sink through the puffy white clouds above, changing them from white to pink or even orange as dusk sets in. All my new friends have disappeared to their homes for the night. I decide to have a quick doze before Mother comes home.

What's that noise? Waking suddenly, my ears prick up. I'm ready and alert for every tiny sound or foreign movement. I hear footsteps. They are coming closer, shuffling up the driveway. At the same time, the sun gradually disappears for another day. There is another sound, one I am becoming familiar with: the jingle of rattling keys. The back door opens. It's Mother.

Opening the door, she lets me inside before plonking her bags down and collapsing straight onto the lounge, her face drained. Her eyes close with exhaustion. It must have been a long day for Mother. I remember what George told me earlier about Mother being tired a lot of the time. I guess today is one of those days. I sniff as I walk up to her. I notice a strange, stale smell on her clothes. It smells like a train. No wonder she is tired. I feel relief now that she is home, safe and sound.

Beneath her blankets, Mother curls up like a cocoon. Lying motionless, her head is deeply pressed into a large cushion, like she is hoping not to be seen. She looks like she will never move again. The television is left on, in case she wakes up, showing one of her favourite programs. Perhaps I can tell Mother all about the episode she missed out on when she does wake. I go off to bed. Awaking from my slumber in the middle of the night, slowly creeping and tip-toeing, not wanting to wake Mother, I detect she hasn't moved. The television is now silent. Opening her eyes, she quietly calls out.

'Teida, everything's all right. I had a big day at work today. You are a good girl. Thank you for checking on me.' She begins patting me and gives me a kiss on the top of my head. Feeling satisfied, I return to bed, knowing Mother is alive and well.

On occasions, Mother comes home way past my bedtime. On these days, I stay outside longer, way after dark, falling asleep near the back door. Being involved with the emergency service, she helps George with all the administrative and financial paperwork. Then George drives Mother home, says a quick hello, and goes home safely to his family. Their relationship isn't romantic, but Mother and George have a special bond, an inner connection, and are the best of friends. They are always there for each other, sharing a lot together and enjoying each other's company. They talk about all kinds of things, even sensitive and personal stuff, thinking no one is listening, but I can understand every word.

Judging by Mother's long work days, it seems that she never had a dog before because she didn't think she would have time to take care of them. *Is Mother someone who stays at home or does she travel like Linda and I did?* Linda and I traveled to many places across town. I slept everywhere when I was with Linda, including in a tent, under the bed and even in the car. *What will happen if Mother does go away and I am left home alone? Who can she ask to look after me? Will it be George? How will I behave with other people visiting that I haven't met?*

I hope they like me.

CHAPTER 6

MY PAW

What's all that commotion? Checking it out, I roam to the front door to find dogs yapping. Many people and dogs are going for their morning stroll on both sides of the street. I even see the dog I saw the other afternoon, but he doesn't seem interested in me today. At the same time, a car drives by and slows down as it nears our home. *Is it George? It can't be. The car is going the opposite way. He must be busy today.*

I bark a good morning greeting and tell the dogs to quieten down. Then I limp back slowly to my mat and lie down. I wonder if Mother knows I am not walking properly and how much pain I am in.

Mother rushes to the telephone as it rings. 'Hello?'

A pause while she listens to the person on the other end.

'Hi George, how are you? Thank goodness you called. Teida's limping. She isn't putting her paw on the floor. Have you noticed? What do I do?'

Mother hangs up the telephone, scratching her head, and walks away. *Was she just talking to George? What was it about? I thought I heard her say 'George', then my name.* Perhaps I am just hearing things.

Later, a familiar car pulls up outside. It is George. He did come over after all. 'Teida!' This time, it is George's deep voice calling me. I can see him waving something in his hand. *My blue leash! Are we going for a walk somewhere?*

'What have you done to your paw Teida? Are you limping?'

With Linda, I had so much fun no matter what we did. It was the enjoyment of just being together, whether it was running in the park, playing fetch, or just lazing about. Now I am excited to go have fun with my new friend as he holds my leash like we're about to have an adventure.

'Teida, come here. I need to put the leash on you. Once I put the leash on you, Mother and I are taking you for a drive.'

–*Wow! A drive in your car! Where are we going George?*

George attaches the leash to my collar and holds it tight in his hand as we all walk outside. 'You are a strong girl, aren't you? Wait on,' George tells me. Down the steps, we turn left, heading towards George's car parked in the driveway. As he opens the back section of his car, without thinking I jump straight in, sore paw and all. Before I know it George closes the boot. Mother and George get in, and we drive off. I wonder where Mother, George and I are going?

George's car is much bigger than Linda's. In Linda's car, I used to sit in the front seat next to her, but the back section of George's car is much more spacious. I have it all to myself. I can sprawl out without bumping into anything, or I can sit up and have a look out of the window. I peer outside and watch the many cars whizzing by, faster and faster. In the background George has the radio on and music plays from the speakers, some of it fast, and some of it slow. I remember some of the music from when I was with Linda. Then George changes his mind and fishes about with his free hand.

'This is the new Pavarotti CD I was telling you about,' George tells Mother as a song begins.

'He is a good opera singer isn't he?' says Mother.

–*He has a deep voice George!*

We turn a corner and come to a sudden stop as George parks the car. George opens the door and I jump out, George holding onto my leash and Mother walking by his side.

Unfamiliar odours capture my attention as we enter the building ahead of us. Unknown animals, mainly cats and dogs, surround me from all sides. Now I realize where they are taking me – the vet! Sitting among other people with their sick and injured animals, all I want to do is leave. I am shaking and panting nervously in anticipation of what may happen next. Finally, it is our turn.

'Teida, would you like to come into this consulting room?' A man in a white coat gestures for George to follow him.

George, taking hold of my leash, follows him into a small room where there are many different smells of dogs that have come and gone. The man closes the door, looks down and presses my paw.

—*Ahhh! Why did he do that?* I yelp out in pain.

'Teida's foot is swollen and infected. That is why she is limping,' I hear the man tell Mother and George. 'Although the thorn is out Teida needs to take some antibiotics so she can walk properly,' the vet says.

He gives Mother some tablets for me to take and we leave and go home. Eventually I am able to run on all fours again.

Pulling up into the driveway George starts whistling a tune. Springing like a rabbit, I jump over the back section, into the middle section where the back seats are and finally land in George's lap. Turning off the ignition, he looks straight at me. 'Teida, what in the hell are you doing here?'

I guess he didn't know that when people whistle, and I am not tied down, I come straight to them as if they are calling my name. Fortunately, we are safe in Mother's driveway.

Home again! We all get out of the car. Slowly, I limp to the backyard, where I stumble over a bright green tennis ball. Mother and George follow close behind. There is no way my paw is going to stop me playing. Instantly taking hold of the ball in my mouth, I scamper up and down before dropping the it at George's feet.

'Since you were so good at the vet today, we will play a game or two of ball.' Picking up the slobbery wet ball, George tosses it with all his might across the yard. With my strong jaw wrapped around it, the ball isn't round anymore.

Is George all right? He looks breathless. It seems he has used all his energy taking me to the vet and then playing a game or two of ball. After a while George gets his breath back and he and Mother go out, leaving me outside with my new ball.

'Teida, Mother and I are going out to buy some lunch. We won't be long,' George tells me.

An appetizing smell enters the house as they return not long after. My tummy growls furiously. *Some lunch for me? What can it be?* The smell of hot chips fills my nostrils as I wait in anticipation.

George calls me over. 'Teida! Come here. Try this.' Approaching him, I see a chip dangling from his fingers. I take it from him gently, then snap it up. Delicious!

SUNDAY MORNING

Birds chirp their morning song as they fly across the cloudless sky or sit way up high in surrounding gum trees. Squawking, singing, shrilling and cooing; each one has some call to add to the chorus. Many birds glide on the wind, moving in time to the natural melodies. Rays of morning sunshine start a brand new day.

A high-pitched piercing sound startles me, noisier as it gets closer. Inside with Mother, I jump up and begin to bark. Following this shrieking sound, I romp from one end of the house to the other. Hurriedly, Mother goes out the front. She returns not long after, holding a newspaper in her hand. Leaving the front door open and the wire door shut I see what all the commotion is about. Blowing a whistle and pushing a wheelbarrow of newspapers along the street is a young boy. Dressed in their pajamas the neighbours approach him from all directions. Do you like the high-pitched sound of a whistle? Being so sensitive to this sound, it is not one of my favourites. Finally, the whistling fades into the background as the boy disappears.

The sound of running water now penetrates my ears. Is it raining inside? 'Teida! Teida, come here.' *That's Mother's voice! What she is up to?'*

Curious to find out, I follow the sound of her voice and find Mother in the bathroom. By this time, the running water has stopped, and I don't see any rain.

'Teida, you can enter the bathroom today. I am going to give you a bath. Do you like having a bath?'

—A bath, do I really need to have a wash? I wonder why Mother doesn't wash me outside. Slowly and cautiously, with my tail in between my legs, I enter the bathroom … and walk straight out again. The tiles are cold and slippery, so different to the carpets and rugs throughout the other parts of our home.

'Come on Teida; you can come here. I've been told you are terrified of the hose, so instead I want to share my bath with you. You are safe here.'

Listening to Mother, still with my tail in between my legs, I slowly walk back into the bathroom. Taking hold, Mother lifts me with both hands up and over the side of the tub. *Boy, Mother is strong, isn't she?* Gently putting me down on the other side, I feel my paws covered with warm water. I start to relax.

Straight from the shower nozzle, jets of warm water wet my body all over. I scramble towards the back of the bath.

'There's no need to be afraid Teida! The water won't hurt you.'

Caressing fingers massage my fur. Mother moves forward so she can reach my back and tail area. Frothy shampoo makes bubbles in the water as I totally relax, floating away into paradise. My neck, back, tail and even my tummy get a wash before Mother rinses me off with refreshing, clean water. Then, taking my feet one at a time, she rubs her fingers through each paw. Looking down, I notice how brown and dirty the water has become.

'That wasn't too bad, was it Teida? Now you are nice and clean. Just wait there while I pull the plug out and empty the bath. Then I will lift you out and take you outside to dry off in the sun.'

Rushing down the plug hole, the gurgling water slowly empties out of the bath. Some of my moulting, loose fur blocks the plughole and Mother pulls it away. Finally, the water disappears. In the meantime, Mother puts my collar back around my neck and places my wet towel on the floor. Carefully lifting me out, Mother ensures I stand on my towel so I do not slip over. Then she puts my leash on and we go outside.

Specks of water fly everywhere as I shake myself dry.

'Here is a bone for you Teida. I have to go back inside and clean up the bathroom. I won't be long then I'll be out with you soon.'

Chomping on a bone Mother has thrown onto the grass to keep me occupied, I feel the bright, warm sunlight drying me off in an instant. A vision of beauty appears in front of me with the many free-spirited, lively, and colorful butterflies fluttering their wings before landing on thin flower stems and taking off again. Some are pale blue like the sky with black lacy edges, others are jet black with white spotted tips, and then there are the delicate pearl white ones. They drift around, deciding which flower they want to land on next. Suddenly, an orange and black striped butterfly appears out of nowhere. This butterfly balances upside down on the stem, determined to reach the pollen deep within the flowers of the garden bed. Its weeping branches sway in time with the wind. Mother returns outside not long after.

'I'm going to do some gardening Teida. Do you want to come and help me? I need to clear out all these weeds from the garden bed here so the flowers can grow.'

Kneeling down on her hands and knees, with a large green bucket by her side, Mother kneads the dirt like a loaf of bread. She is now as tall as me. Mother fills up the bucket with overgrown weeds, unwanted grass and fallen branches. Many rambling stems are clinging and strangling plants hidden underneath that are striving for the sun. I watch close by. *There's my white ball. No wonder I couldn't find it. I wonder what other discoveries I can make.*

—*Here Mother! Look what I found*, I say, as I drop the white ball in front of her, trying to get her attention. *Let's have some fun. Play with me for a while, then go back and finish what you are doing.*

We play some ball as Mother takes a breather.

'Thanks Teida. I needed to have a break. Today is a good day for gardening, so I'd better continue now and finish weeding this section. Thank you for keeping me company and helping me out. We will play more ball when I finish. I won't be long.'

Has Mother noticed my contribution to the garden? Does she appreciate all my effort fertilizing? When Mother is out for a while, I fertilize the plants instead of the grass, encouraging them to flourish. This means Mother needs to be careful in the garden, particularly where she steps or puts her hand, especially near the roses and lemon tree.

With sweat dripping from her brow mixed with the black grains of earth, Mother continues. The dirt becomes engrained within her fingers. Piles of garden waste fill up all the large buckets surrounding her. She stands and turns on the tap, washing her hands clean before grabbing the long rubbery green hose. Totally absorbed in her thoughts, she waters the garden and rinses off her hands at the same time. In the meantime, I find a way of escaping to the other end of the yard. Another ball lands at my feet.

—*Where did that come from? Has it just fallen from the sky?*

'Teida, I have finished now. Let's play some ball. Bring me the ball.'

Looking at Mother wanting to play, I feel hesitation. How do I get back to her with the water coming from the hose? If only the water came out a different way, like rain does from the sky.

WHAT A SMALL WORLD

A few months have now passed since leaving Linda. What is she doing now? Does she regret her decision to give me away?

During this time, other people have come to Mother's home wanting to meet me – Annie's new pet.

'Teida, my parents are coming over today. They want to meet you. You will like them. Eventually, you will meet all my family, my brothers and sister, too.'

There's a knock at the door.

'Hello Annie, where are you?' Two people enter that I haven't seen before. Two older people, a lady and a man, standing upright with their heads held high. Walking through to the backyard, they follow Mother to the other end of the garden, almost scraping their heads against the clothes line. *So these people are Annie's mother and father.* Now I see where she gets her height.

'Teida, these are my parents. You will often see them pop over and visit.'

'So this is Teida,' Annie's dad says, looking down at me.

'Welcome Teida, we have heard a lot about you, all good things, of course,' says Annie's mother, bending down to pet me.

I notice a particular scent surrounding the lady, telling me she has a pet dog of her own. 'Teida is a beautiful dog. She seems to fit right in. She likes you Annie.'

I look up at Annie's parents and wag my tail.

'Annie, where do you keep your plastic bags?' her dad asks.

Mother goes inside and gets a couple of plastic bags and gives them to her dad. I watch, intrigued.

After tucking one plastic bag inside the other, he finds a small garden trowel and walks up and down the lawn, cleaning up my fertilizer. Now I understand.

'All clean now,' he says.

'Thanks, Dad,' Mother replies.

Both of Annie's parents have brown to black hair and eyes as dark as coal that light up when they smile. Annie's mother helps prune back the overgrown shrubs, and her dad weeds underneath. They all chat about the variety of plants within each of the garden beds. *Now I know what those small yellow flowers are called that are peeping up amongst the small strapping leaves. Daffodils!* Now all the gardening is complete; they sit down to have a cool glass of water on the back deck. Now I can see where Mother gets her gardening talents and knowledge from.

A few weeks later, a serene, quiet lady and two stylish younger men come to visit. My eyes peer upwards as they all tower above me. *Have I seen this lady before?* She does look familiar. Her brown eyes sparkle as they gaze in my direction.

'Teida, I want to introduce you to my brothers and my sister.'

'Hello Teida, you're looking well. How are you settling in?' the lady asks. Redirecting her conversation towards Mother, she says 'Teida's settling in great Annie.'

The sound of her voice, I have heard it before. Animals are great at reading people through their energy field. They immediately tune into their surroundings, recognizing familiarity or something strange or unusual.

Now let me think. Hmmm! I reminisce back to my days with Linda. *Now I remember!* She used to dog sit me when Linda went away on weekends or during the holidays.

'Teida,' she calls. *Yes, that is the voice I remember from all those years ago.* Her arms are held open wide. I run towards her before we reunite together in one big hug. Waking up early, she would let me out of the laundry so I could be by her side. I had free run of the house in those days. *Millie did say to me earlier that I have met Annie's sister before, and she was right.*

What a small world. I didn't realize she was part of Annie's family, but now I notice that they have lots in common. Long and flowing brunette hair trails behind her, blowing in the summer breeze. Her complexion and appearance are similar to Annie's, even their height. I can understand how people get them mixed up. They look so much like twins. I wonder who is older? Everything is now falling into place. I realize now who that first phone call was to, who Linda was talking to that day we went for a drive together for the last time.

From this I make an observation. Just like dogs, humans have a mother and father as well as brothers and sisters. We all have families. Like dogs, it appears humans have a pack too. Humans have a group of people who care about each other and provide each other with a sense of belonging. They are there in good times and bad times wanting to lend a hand, similar to how my mama was there for me as a tiny young pup.

I remember the last time I saw Mama. It was my afternoon nap, and was I curled up to Mama, pressing my nose against her belly as she laid stretched out on her side. Then suddenly many shadows appeared over me, larger and larger as they came closer. My ears perked up, ready for action. Mama came forward and rigidly stood before me with alarm. I remained behind her, tucked away, hidden against my Mama's body and clinging tightly. Then, after slowly calming down, my mama's tongue licked me for the last time. Her maternal instincts from the prior experiences with my siblings being taken away knew it was time to say goodbye to me too. That was the moment I met Linda. She lifted me up in the palm of her hand, put me into a small dark box and took me away. Linda was the first human I ever interacted with. She took me to puppy obedience class so I could learn how to mix with humans as well as dogs.

Being part of a human family, dogs rely on their human owner to communicate to us and provide leadership and guidance on how they expect us to behave within their environment. The human must take care of their pet in a respectful and nurturing way, treating us how they would like to be treated. We as dogs do not care if our owner is rich or poor, educated or illiterate, clever or dull. Pets do not judge: we just want to be included as part of a household. We are keen to always share in our owner's happiness, sadness or whatever the day brings.

Once dogs are separated from their siblings, we don't know the location of our family. More often than not, we are unable to reunite with our brothers or sisters. *I wonder what my siblings are up to these days. Do they have owners who treat them well and give them a sense of belonging? Are they still alive? Do any of them live close by? Would I recognize them if they walked past me, in the street, at the local vet, or in the park? Do they look like me? Are they similar to me in personality?*

We all played together as young pups with our mama, without a care in the world, except for being nervous of the older man we lived with. His cold, frightening eyes were constantly glaring in our direction. Numerous wrinkles emphasized his every expression. His pipe filled the air with smoke, day in, day out. Smoke covered our fur. As we walked from one corner to the other on the cold cement, bits of dirt and tobacco became wedged between our paws. Then, one by one, we were all given away. When my brother was taken, there was barking, whimpering and crying. Mama and I were left behind to fend for ourselves, surrounded by four gray concrete walls.

What has happened to my mama? I still wonder today, being the last pup of the litter to find a new home, why Mama could not come with me to Linda's instead of being left behind on her own. I would have liked Annie and George to meet my dog family. Yet that's the difference between dogs and humans.

Having many opportunities, humans are able to catch up on what they are up to by making time to write, visit or talk on the phone. I often see Mother communicate with people who mean a lot to her. From the people who come to say hello to Mother, I gain knowledge of who her family and friends are. Each car has its own sound. Each person has their own footsteps.

UNEXPECTED EVENTS

M ore time passes, and I am now getting used to the routines of the day. But one day, leaving for work, Mother catches the train early in the morning and closes the door behind her. *Why did Mother forget to put me outside? Do I have to stay inside all day until she comes home?* There is no grass to run on, no birds to chase, not even any toys to play with.

I listen out with my sharp doggie ears for sounds from outside. Scraping of the side gate being opened and closed. Vibrating sounds of a lawnmower, moving back and forth. I remember Mother saying something about the lawn being mowed, so perhaps that is why she left me inside today. *Who is outside? Is it George?* Not long afterwards, I hear the sound of George's car. Opening the front door he walks inside. 'Hello Teida,' George says, giving me a pat to say hello. 'I have to go outside for a minute. I won't be long.'

The lawnmower is still making a noise in the background. Well, if it is not George outside, who is mowing the lawn?

Leaving me inside, George goes to the front yard. Finally, after what seems like an eternity, the noise stops. *Where is George? Has he forgotten about me? Why hasn't he returned?* Jumping onto the lounge and peering out, my head reaches the transparent glass of the large window facing the front yard. Squeezing between the blinds, I see George standing face to face with another man. His mouth is moving. *What is he saying?* They stop talking, and the other man leaves. Quickly I climb down before George sees me up here. Snap! My paw catches on the blind cord. *Oh No! What have I done? I hope I don't get into trouble.*

George returns. 'Sorry I took so long outside Teida. A man came to mow Annie's lawn and I had to give him some money. The grass out the back is much shorter and easier for you to run around on now.' George notices what happened. 'Don't worry about the blind cord; it can be fixed. Let's go outside and play ball.'

Silently, we walk out to the backyard.

'Here Teida; go get the ball.'

Hmm! Something tells me George is not well today. He carefully lowers himself into the chair and pauses before skyrocketing the ball across one side of the yard to the other.

—*Here George*, I say as I return the ball to his feet.

This time George bowls the ball underarm along the concrete footpath between the grass and the garden bed.

—*George, are you all right? You do not have as much energy as you normally do. You seem much more tired today.*

'Teida, that's enough, I have to go now. I'm not too well today. I had a migraine last night. I need to go home and lie down.'

Slowly rising, keys in one hand and picking up his belongings on the way, he departs, closing the back door before going out the front. He drives away.

The powerful fragrance of the freshly cut lawn and churned earth surrounds me. Where I tread, the thin blades of grass are lighter and softer. My pathway creation appears larger, more noticeable and bigger in size. In the center, Mother's clothesline is radiating many artistic shadows. The shrubs are throwing shade as I romp from one side of the yard to the other.

Weeks go by. Another work day arrives. 'Hi Teida.' That's George's voice as he unlocks the front door. George seems a lot better than the last time he came over when Mother was at work.

I bolt to the front door at the sound of a knock at the door, barking. 'That's the handyman Teida. We need to get a quote to have some repairs done in the backyard,' George tells me as he opens the front door.

On the other side, I see an unfamiliar face. George immediately directs him around to the backyard. 'Would you mind walking along the side of the house to the backyard? I'll meet you there.'

As the man enters the backyard and with me in tow, George closes the side gate. Standing beside George, observing his every move, I notice George's finger pointing downward to a spot on the deck. The conversation is about repairing the deck area. Giving George a piece of paper, the other man leaves.

Out of nowhere the world starts spinning around in front of me and an overwhelming shortness of breath sends me panting for air. Blurriness, as if I am looking underwater. Fuzziness, as I try to see my friend George standing nearby on the back deck. My legs have turned rubbery and feel like jelly, yet my body seems to be as stiff as a board. Trembling and shaking uncontrollably. *Oh no! I am having a seizure. How do I tell George what is happening? How do I tell him my symptoms and how I am feeling? Do Mother and George know about my epilepsy?* Like humans, dogs have seizures too and can be epileptic. I have been having fits since I was about five years old.

I hear the large deck chair being pushed and dragged backwards. I see a lot more space in front of me. But I cannot see George. I can hear his voice, yet it is so far away. *Where is he? Has George disappeared?* I do not want to be left on my own in this state.

Eventually, a soothing, calm energy comes over me. Surrounding warmth and tenderness; telling me not to panic. My breathing finally slows down from its rapid rate. Turning my face, I see George. Instantly I know. George *has* dealt with urgent situations before. I guess that is from his experience in the emergency service. Without panicking, he knew exactly what to do. He understood what has just happened. No more being scared, no more shaking. My normal world returns. *Phew! What a relief!* I can balance on my four legs again, walking forward. I can even see George. He never left me. I immediately go straight up to George as he starts talking to me.

'Teida, it is George here. You just had a seizure. Have a drink of water and take things slowly. You will be all right now.' George gives me a pat. 'Linda told Annie and me that on occasions you have epileptic seizures.'

Lick! Lick!

—*Thank you George, for your patience, for caring, and for just being with me. I was scared and unsure if you knew I am epileptic.* This seizure only lasted a few minutes. However, to me, a few minutes is such a long time. These seizures appear every four months or so at any time, day or night.

Exhausted and thirsty from the whole ordeal, slowly I walk to my red bucket. My tongue is lapping up the ice cold water. Before long, I am back to my normal self again. George puts everything back in its original spot, then says his goodbyes.

I hear Mother's grandma Millie coming over.

—*Teida, are you all right?*

—*Millie, I feel so much better now. It is so reassuring that George was here.*

—*George has a lot of knowledge about anything and everything. He is a very wise man. George watched over you and was not going to leave until he knew you were back on all fours again.*

—*I look forward to being inside and sleeping in my cozy bed. My bed is so toasty and warm. So different to when I was a wee pup sleeping with my dog mama and siblings. We were all together in a small basket containing some torn blankets, hidden in a back corner behind a desolate old car. No light entered. We were in total darkness day and night, surrounded by four gray concrete walls. It's nice to have somewhere safe and comfy to go after a tough day.*

—*It won't be long Teida; Mother is on her way home from work. George told her all about what happened today.*

CHAPTER 9

Soon after my conversation with Millie, Mother walks inside with a look of relief on her face, approaching me with a big hug and a pat before I go to bed and off to sleep. All of a sudden, morning is here, and Mother is off to work once again.

STORMY SKIES

S haking uncontrollably, eyes darting, my tail hidden tucked between my legs. My internal barometer wants to forewarn Mother of an impending thunderstorm coming to descend over the neighborhood. This time though, she isn't home.

—*Where are you Mother?*

Dark and daunting violet clouds move across the sky. Looking up to the heavens, I see thick sheets of icy water plummeting down. It gushes over the rooftops like a huge waterfall, making many puddles below. Bucketing down in all directions, the rain makes its way onto the back deck. Drooping garden plants, distressed and sorrowful, drowning from the heavy volumes of water filling up the garden beds. If only I could help. Percussion sounds of the echoing thunder, so powerful, like the angry bellowing roar of a lion. I can almost feel the vibration thump against my chest as it comes closer.

Dazzling thin bolts of lightning sparkle in the night sky. Flash! The spark is so bright it hurts my eyes.

—*I'm scared. I need Mother. I want to be inside.*

Muddy sopping pathways, the water unable to escape. Leaves are dripping, holding on for dear life as their stems are pulled down with the heavy weight of the downpour. The lime green carpet of grass is so thirsty, absorbing so much water. All of Mother's pot plants, large and small, are spread out on the concrete pathways hoping to grab a drink too. Plastic buckets at the edge of the deck are filling up with the water falling over the roof edge. Meanwhile, I lie hiding close to the back door, hoping to stay dry and soon to be inside together with Mother.

Squally winds blowing trees from side to side. Standing strong, their roots implanted, determined not to move. Falling twigs snap off the debris flying around. Branches are pulled up and down, confused by which direction the wind is swirling. Even a branch from the large tree in the front yard left its trunk, landing at my feet. The sound of the chimes become louder and deeper as the wind becomes stronger. Garden ornaments fall over, some of them breaking as they land in the garden beds. The wind blows the rain closer to me as I stay sheltered on the back deck. Shivering and trembling, I stay still.

Finally, there is a break in the skies. The strong winds turn into a gentle breeze. *Phew! What a relief!* Before crawling underneath the house to escape from the loud rumbling vibrations above, I quickly dash onto the grass and find the driest part to squat in, but to no avail. My paws seem to disappear from underneath me, sinking further into the wet lawn.

Pitter patter, splattering rain beats against the window pane. Small droplets slide down the windows like snails, leaving their trails behind. Beautiful harmonies emerge from the gentle rain, playing tunes on the rooftops. Tiny raindrops are bouncing off the garden path as the fairies of nature splash around in the freedom of their own world. Leaves gently dance on the ground. Taking a deep breath I find the air is now clean and refreshed. I smell the remnants left over from the rain. All the dirt and bad odours have been washed away. The surrounding colors of the lawn and vegetation are captivating; I never knew there were so many shades of green. Slowly but surely, all the creatures reappear, peeping up through the earth, showing their glory to the universe. They have survived too.

Drowned like a rat, my fur dripping, feeling gluggy all over. My blackened paws are covered with mud. *What do I do? I can't have Mother see me like this*. I flick my fur from one side to the other. Water flies in every direction. I brush against each blade of grass, which seems to grow as it catches my feet. Under the house, I lay cozy amongst the sandy gravel and dirt in the hope of drying off a bit more. Finally, Mother comes home. I race from beneath the house and wait eagerly at the back door. Touching me with her cold, dry hands, she finds I am sopping wet all over.

'Teida look! You are all wet from the rain. Wait here. I will get a towel and wipe you down.'

Soon Mother returns.

She wraps a large, soft, pink towel around my dripping wet body, the mud turning the towel from pink to grimy black. 'Now Teida, I need to use your drinking water to clean your paws and legs before you go inside. You really got muddy from the storm, didn't you? We will be inside soon where it will be nice and warm.'

Mother lifts my paws one by one and dunks them in the clear, cool water.

—*Brrr! That's cold Mother.* Each clump, each build-up of mud falls away. Mother rubs my feet between her hands, one paw at a time, which quickly warms me up. Dabbing my face with my green face washer, Mother reveals my original complexion. Although still wet from head to toe, I am dirt-free.

'Come on Teida; you can go inside. I know you were wet, but now you are nice and clean.' Mother opens the back door. *If only I could clean and wash myself.*

Barrelling off, I race up and down the hallway in excitement. Pounding paws on the floor. Joyful barking filling the air. Round and round in circles I go, non-stop; from the lounge room to the dining room through the kitchen, flicking the ends of the kitchen rug before I am greeted by the warm woollen blankets and the comfort of my own bed. After feeling so exhausted, I collapse in a heap, sleeping safe and dry.

Suddenly my dream is interrupted by the sound of a car driving over the pebbles, making its way under the car port. With it being totally dark it seems like the middle of the night. I can still hear the rain tumbling outside. Slowly stirring, stretching and shaking I open my eyes and make a mad dash to the door, knowing who is coming to visit. Slow, shuffling footsteps steadily approach, climbing the three steps one at a time. I stand, wagging my tail. I wait for what seems like an eternity. Why is it taking so long for this person to approach the door? Finally, with the front door already open, he enters.

I am right. It is my friend George. Even after my bedtime, I always make sure I see him, even if it is for a short time before I go back to sleep.

Today though, George looks unusually pale and tired, weak and worn out from his head right down to his motley legs and toes, which do not want to hold him up. Perhaps he has had a hard day. There seems to be a lot on his mind. I hear George talking to Mother about one thing, then quickly changing the subject to something else, so that I find it hard to keep up.

George finally makes it to his favourite blue lounge. He takes off his jacket and sits down. The dripping water from George's jacket falls onto my fur.

'Hello Teida, I didn't expect to see you up so late. I thought you would be asleep,' George comments, giving me a pat on the top of my head.

'George, do you want a cup of coffee? Don't forget you need to test your sugar.'

'Coffee, yes please.' As Mother puts the kettle on George gets a square shaped object out of his bag. Something I haven't seen before. He pricks his finger, and I see a drop or two of blood being put onto a small stick. The stick is then inserted into the square machine.

'Sugar, 3.4; I need something to eat.'

From George using his device to test his sugar, I discover George is diabetic. *Poor George!* No wonder he isn't too well, with his sugar count being so low and needing something to eat so late at night, when normally it is time for sleeping. Perhaps that is the cause of his motley legs too. Now I know why when George pops over during the day he helps himself to a biscuit or two.

Mother brings over George a cup of coffee and gives him a slice of her homemade cake.

—*Can I have some too Mother?*

Almost half an hour later, after drinking his cup of coffee and eating some cake, color returns to George's face, and he appears to be much stronger. With the rain easing to a soft sprinkle George stands up, says goodbye, and leaves to go home.

'Remember to give three rings of your phone when you get home George, so I know you are home safe and sound.'

Mother says goodnight to me, turns off the lights, and gets ready for bed, while I go back to my bed and off to sleep.

All of a sudden the lights are turned on again and we are woken by a sudden high-pitched continuous sound as the security alarm beeps loudly.

'Oh no,' Mum says in a panic.

—*Mother what's wrong?*

'My landline telephone doesn't work. All due to the storm. Now I have to put up with the security alarm beeping all night and won't get any sleep, and I am waiting for George to call me.'

Mother's mobile phone rings.

'Yeah, the landline doesn't work George. I have no credit on my mobile so can you call the phone company and let them know. I'm scared George. I hear flapping against my bedroom window. I hope the branches of the tree don't fall.'

Mother finishes talking to George. Meanwhile, the beeping of the alarm continues in the background.

'Teida I don't like this rain and howling wind. It is all getting too much for me.' Mother starts to cry. 'I'm going to sleep on the lounge tonight Teida.'

The beeping stops, and I hear Mother softly breathing. She is now asleep.

HAVING FUN AND DOING TRICKS

Half-expecting gray skies left over from yesterday's storm, instead I am welcomed by rays of sunlight as a blanket of white cotton wool disappears. Thin silky strands in the shape of a wheel come into view, delicately hanging from the many shrubs in our garden and even the clothesline. It appears Mrs Spider and her friends have been busy throughout the night with their creations all throughout the garden, high and low. Each individual cobweb is uniquely designed, with beads of water from the recent rain glistening like crystals.

—*Good morning Teida. Nice day isn't it?*

—*Hello, Mrs Spider, how did you survive the heavy rain yesterday? Your webs are very shiny today.*

—*Thank you Teida, they were cleaned thoroughly by the rain while we spiders hid beneath the branches of the trees and shrubs.*

—*Good morning Teida.* This time the voice is from below me. It appears to be coming from the leafy bushes in Mother's garden.

I see Sally Snail peering out from the bushes. Looking left and right, she cautiously comes out in the warm sun to dry her shell off.

—*Hello Sally Snail, how are you after the big storm? I am so relieved the rain didn't drown you.*

—*That is what my shell is for Teida. It keeps me protected and dry. I am out to find something soft and sweet to eat. The rain softens all the leaves and makes it easier for us snails to munch and absorb the many flavors of each plant. I am so pleased you survived the storm Teida. What are you doing today?*

—*It is a good day to be out in the glorious sunshine and spend time with Mother when she returns from doing some shopping. Look at how shiny and clean my toys are. The rain has cleaned them all for me.*

—*Your toys are bright and shiny Teida, just like our cobwebs,* says Mrs Spider.

The back door opens, interrupting our conversation.

—*Hello George, I wasn't expecting you today. Look at all the shopping. Bags and bags of groceries all over the floor, I don't know how Mother would have carried all this shopping home on her own.*

With all the excitement of being inside with Mother and George, pinning my ears back I gallop up and down, round and round in circles like a small horse, going from the kitchen to the lounge room and back again. Bending down on his hands and knees, George begins to creep closer towards me. At the same time, in a deep voice, he says, 'Slowly I turn. Step … by … step.

Closer. Closer.' Upon reaching me, he pounces. He attempts to tackle me, before I escape from his grasp, running around more and more. Then I suddenly stop, sitting face to face in front of him, smiling from ear to ear. A new game is now invented.

'Teida!' I approach George, sitting on his favourite chair, tapping his legs simultaneously. 'Teida, cuddle.' George repeats himself in a friendly and encouraging tone as I wander up to him.

'Teida! Come here! Cuddle!' George taps his legs a second time. Jumping up, instinctively I wrap my two front legs around his lap. I am given a pat and our eyes connect. *Now I understand what George is teaching me. A way to give someone a cuddle.*

I sneak my head up higher, licking George just under his chin and at the same time catching his whiskers. 'That tickles!' Sitting on the floor or on the lounge, Mother joins in and, like George, asks me to cuddle too. I intertwine my legs around her. Like George, she gives me lots of pats and hugs.

With songs playing in the background on the stereo system, Mother decides to show me a new trick. As a tune is playing, I hear Mother's voice saying 'Teida!' and simultaneously tapping her hands up and down on her lap. Approaching her, automatically I place my front paws into her open hands. Holding my paws and taking control, supporting my back, Mother moves my front paws from side to side or back and forth, waltzing together in time with the music. This is how I dance!

On the subject of music, perhaps I could be in a band someday, performing in front of many people or dogs. When a song with a good beat is playing, Mother calls me. 'Teida, come here.' Listening to Mother, I walk towards her.

'Sit Teida; I want to try something with you.' Once I sit down, Mother takes my paws as if I am dancing. Taking hold, Mother moves my front paws one at a time to the beat of the music. Up and down, sometimes fast and sometimes slow. *Perhaps I am playing the drums or being the conductor of an orchestra.*

Besides teaching me new tricks, how about the other way around? Have you heard of a dog playing tricks on their owner? This is so much fun. Believe it or not, I play tricks on Mother and George all the time. Let me tell you about what happened one Christmas.

Pretending to be Santa Claus, peering over I saw George sneak something under the Christmas tree, a large, bright pink tennis ball. Stopping in his tracks, he changes his mind. Maybe he saw me watching him.

'Teida, I know it isn't Christmas yet. I may not see you at Christmas, so I am going to give you your Christmas present early. Here Teida, have a look at this. It is a large tennis ball that should last you a while. Shall we have a game?'

We start playing.

—*Thank you George.* It would be too long for a dog to wait until Christmas time.

George tosses the ball, and I grab it in my mouth, holding it with my jaw, before dropping the ball in front of George all in one piece.

'That's right Teida; this ball is much stronger than the smaller tennis balls you have had.'

Christmas comes and goes. George was right. He wasn't able to pop over at Christmas. A few days after Christmas he comes over for a visit, wanting to play.

'Teida! Let's play ball. Go get your new ball Teida. Where's the ball? Where's the ball Teida?'

With all the other toys and balls nowhere to be seen on the grass, I know exactly which ball George wants to play with. George wants to play with my new pink ball. The one he gave me for Christmas. I stand looking blankly at him.

'Teida! Where's the ball?'

Mother watches from inside. I can see her standing at the kitchen sink. She must be making George a cup of coffee. She comes outside puts George's cup of coffee on the table.

'Do you know where Teida's ball is? Has she chewed it up already?' George asks Mother with some annoyance in his voice.

'Not that I am aware of,' Mother responds.

'Teida, what have you done with your new ball? You couldn't have destroyed it already!'

George and Mother wander around looking in the garden beds, searching down the side of the house. They even put their heads underneath the house, rummaging everywhere before eventually give in, resigned to the fact that the pink ball is lost forever.

'We have searched everywhere and can't find the ball Teida, play with this one instead. I'll have to get you another one,' George says, sitting on the bench out on the back deck.

Not long afterwards, I appear from underneath the house holding onto my Christmas present. There is no way I am going to lose such a special toy, one given with so much love. The expressions on their face say it all. George and Mother were in total awe. I was playing another version of hide-and-seek – dog style.

Whether it is a bright pink tennis ball or something else, Mother and George are always on the look out for indestructible dog toys for a dog with a strong, powerful jaw to play with. Of course, the dog toy must not take five minutes to destroy. The stronger the toy, the longer it lasts.

WHAT HAPPENED TO MOTHER?

One cold winter's night, pacing up and down the yard, my heart is pulsating as if I have run a ten-mile hike. I see street lights sending pools of golden light onto the pavement. Shining brightly above, the glistening moon is as bright as the glow of a torch showing me the way. Sparkling stars twinkle like diamonds, allowing me to see my way forward through the pitch-black darkness of the night sky.

Mother is late coming home from work. *Where is she? She is never this late.* My instincts tell me when someone is due home from school or work. *What do I do?*

Patiently I wait. *Is Mother with George? Does he know where Mother is?*

I listen to the nocturnal buzzing and humming of the night insects; the croaking of a frog or two hidden beneath the earth. *I wonder if they know anything?*

Cars drive by. Not one of them stops. There is hardly anyone walking past. The street is so desolate and quiet. All the neighbourhood children are inside. The house lights are switched off. It appears all forms of life are sleeping. No one knocks at the door. It is so silent you can hear a pin drop. Inside the telephone rings and rings before stopping and starting again. No answer. I mustn't be the only one looking for Mother.

I decide to search, sniffing alongside the fence and giving a bark or two.

—*Does anyone out there know where Mother is? Has Mother fallen over hurting herself walking home from the train station?* Totally distracted I spring off a thin sticky substance, invisible to my eyes, hanging from the top of the deck down onto the branch below. Looking up I see Mrs Spider sitting upright in the center, looking proud of her latest creation.

—*Hello Mrs Spider.*

—*Hello Teida, you are normally inside at this hour, why are you up this late at night?*

—*Mother hasn't come home. I am worried about her. Perhaps I am sleeping out here tonight. Will she come home, Mrs Spider? I'm scared I won't see her anymore. Mrs Spider, have you seen Mother? Do you know where she is?*

—*No I don't Teida. My spider friends and I will keep a look out though. I am sure she isn't too far away. Don't worry Teida; Mother will be home soon and you will be in your warm bed inside.*

Soon after my chat with Mrs Spider, I go to the back door, hoping to hear Mother. Still there is nothing but total silence.

I start howling and whining. Just as I am about to close my eyes, Mother's grandma Millie, who lives in the rose garden, comes over.

—*Teida, there is no need to be upset now. Mother is all right. She is very upset. She has had a really bad day at work, and George is bringing her home. They will be here soon. Have a nap. You will need to be alert and awake for when she returns.*

Listening to Millie, I curl up in a circle on the back door mat, close my eyes and doze off.

I am suddenly woken by a glow shining right in my face. Flashing lights go on and off in the driveway and make their way through the blinds in the window. It seems as if I nodded off for a second, yet and hour or two may have passed. The front door opens, then the back door is unlocked. I see George on the other side. 'Come inside Teida. Sorry it's so late. You must be tired. Mother is here too. She is in the lounge room. I'm putting the kettle on and will be out in a minute.'

—*Mother what happened? You look so sad.*

As I walk closer, I find that a strange odour is coming from Mother's leg. Wanting to lick her leg and make it better I hesitate, knowing there is more. Something else is traumatizing Mother. She takes off her shoes and socks and puts her feet on the coffee table. Her gray trousers are torn and damaged, exposing dried blood and broken skin on her knee. Swollen and inflamed bruising surrounds a large graze. Now I know what the strange odour is.

Did you know that a feature with dogs is they are very sensitive to the environment around them? I recognize smells and can tell when someone is happy or sad, sick or healthy. Our primary sense is our smell. We use our nose to sniff and detect things, close by or even quite a distance away.

Millie was right; Mother did have a bad day. Now she is home I can keep watch and take care of her and soon she will feel much better too. I'm happy George brought Mother home safely.

'Teida I am so sorry you had to stay outside so late, I thought I would be home much earlier,' Mother says, bending over and holding me so tightly. 'I had my half yearly performance review today and it went from mid-afternoon to way into the evening. By the time I had finished everyone else had gone home except my boss and me, and the worst thing is that I have now been made redundant.' Mother pauses to take a breath.

George comes over with a cup of tea for Mother and sits next to her with his cup of coffee.

'It seems Annie's boss never appreciated all her effort,' George says, staring down at the table. 'Those early mornings and late nights, making sure all those deadlines were met and helping out all her clients. I was so worried about Annie's whereabouts that I called her and found her still at work. Being 8:30pm by this stage, I told Annie to get a taxi to the emergency service and that I would take her home. Then on the way home we came across a big car accident on the motorway. A five car pile up. Mangled vehicles, smashed windscreens, people standing to the side. There were no emergency service vehicles, so I had to call for assistance and control the oncoming traffic until the ambulance and police arrived.'

As George takes a sip of his coffee, Mother continues.

'Teida, see my bruised and battered knees. I injured myself tripping over the side of the motorway. I was in the car and

George's mobile phone started to ring. It was an urgent call; I had to get out of the car and give the telephone to George. I stumbled and fell over. There were all these casualties as a result of the accident, and I was injured because I got out of the car to give George his mobile phone.'

Comforting Mother through her ordeal, I sit, nestling myself between her and George. Poor Mother, going through all this. I am so grateful George was able to drive her home.

Blinking quickly, Mother hides the tears about to overflow from her bloodshot eyes. The redness of her wet face glows, showing her grief and anger, wanting to speak the truth; telling her side of the story in the hope someone will listen. Her shoulders are pulled down, as if giant boulders lay there, unable to move. Still the odd tear sneaks out of her despairing eyes. As Mother finishes telling me the events of the day, I hear total relief as well as the exhaustion in her voice, knowing that she is finally home.

Why did Mother lose her job? What will lay ahead for her? No more late nights; no more early mornings. We will spend more time together. Maybe my wish has come true. Mother to spend the rest of her life with me and not work anymore. Little does she know there will be bigger and better things for her on the horizon. Everything happens for a reason. As one door closes another opens. She just has to wait and see.

The crispness of a winter's morning awaits as we both wake from an emotional night.

'Teida. I am going out for a while. You were such a good girl helping me last night. Here is a bone for you to enjoy while I am gone. I won't be too long.'

Thump! Landing outside with a thud, an appetizing bone is thrown onto the back deck as Mother goes out the front door. Standing over it and grabbing hold, I lift the bone onto the lawn. Pulling and tearing, my strong, sharp teeth gnaw through it, crunching and biting until it all disappears.

Looking up, I see Mrs Spider is hanging from above.

—*Hi Teida, what happened last night? Is your Mother all right?*

Climbing down from her webs so high to sit on the stems and branches below, we wait for Mr Worm and Mr Ant who are coming over to hear the story too. Then we all sit together as I share with them the events of the night before.

All of a sudden an indefinable, unrelenting, throbbing echo overpowers me, interrupting our conversation. Rising above the hum of the cars, sounding like a siren inside the house penetrating the sealed windows. My paws just won't reach to cover my ears. All my friends scatter away.

The startled neighborhood dogs all join in, creating a background chorus of howling. Not to be overcome by such a loud volume, I play hide-and-seek, running further away from the sound in the hope it will not follow me. *How long will this last? When is Mother coming home?*

This scary noise brings back memories of when I was a pup, going to obedience class for the first time. I tried to blend into the background while Linda chatted to the other dog owners. Noses came up, touching, prodding and sniffing as many dogs roamed freely. Escaping, I ran as fast as my tiny legs would carry me. Way down to the other end of the classroom where I could go no further.

—*Hello Teida, what are you doing cowering so low?* Austin asks, coming to the back fence and noticing me crouched and trembling underneath the house.

—*The loud noise scares me, Austin. It sounds like it is so close and maybe following me around. Do you know what it could be?*

—*Teida, I have heard similar sounds but not so close. It sounds like an alarm coming from somewhere, maybe inside your home or a car close by.*

—*Do you think it will stop? The sound is hurting my ears.*

Just to be safe, I still stay in my hiding spot underneath the house. Austin sits with me for a while until I calm down. Silence at last!

Not long after I settle down, Mother comes home and lets me inside.

'Oh no, the alarm went off. I will have to reset the security system,' Mother says in an exasperated tone. Later in the day, there is an unexpected knock at the front door. Who could this be? Considering myself as part of the welcoming committee, streaking across from the other side of the room, I arrive at the front door just as Mother opens it.

Standing by Mother's side, an unfamiliar face confronts me. Mother's neighbor, coming over to make sure everything is all right. He must have heard the noise too. *Who else heard it?*

Listening to their conversation, I learn that the loud noise *was* Mother's security system. Something inside had set the alarm off. Mother's neighbor tells her that anything as small as an insect flying around or dust in the alarm system could have triggered the noise.

He also mentions to Mother that he didn't realize she had a dog. When the alarm sounded he had peered over the fence, and I was nowhere to be seen in the backyard.

GEORGE'S HEALTH

Pungent rotten eggs, rotting meat or stagnant water circulating in the air as if flies were around a dead animal. *It can't be eggs. Mother doesn't eat them. What is that horrible stench? Where is it coming from?*

Taking his time, George lowers himself on the arm of his favourite blue lounge. His face says it all. Without words I know. Holding onto Mother's arm he props himself up to stand, then limps as he puts one foot in front of the other to walk outside, before taking a breath and sitting down again.

Our eyes make contact. I lower my cold, wet nose, nuzzling George and licking his bare feet one at a time. The smell lures me. I am determined to locate the distasteful odour that is festering around George.

Faster and faster like a vacuum cleaner, in desperation my nose goes up and down George's motley legs, along his discolored ankles, feet and toes without stopping. Looking down, George watches with anticipation. Sniffing further, I discover George's right foot seems to be smelling stronger than his left. I come to the back of George's foot and stop sniffing. His back right heel just doesn't seem right to me. There is a bandage covering it so I can only assume from the smell that something bad has happened to his foot. Peering upwards, I communicate my observations to George.

—*George I know you are grimacing in pain. What is wrong with your right foot? Your legs and feet seem to be worse today, and your lower right leg and foot smell really bad.*

I hope George understands what I am saying. What can a dog do? Do I have any magical powers to heal someone?

'Teida, you keep sniffing and you are right. My legs are not good today and there is something wrong with my right heel. I have a wound on the back of my heel and it is now infected. Now the wound has become much bigger and is causing pain in my foot. The pain goes up my leg too. The doctors are doing all they can to help me. I have to put on a dressing every day and keep my foot bandaged all the time to prevent further infection. Hopefully, my foot will get better soon.'

Every day and night afterwards my mind keeps ticking. Even though George told me the doctors are doing all they can to help him, something just doesn't seem right. Every time I see George, the smell becomes stronger and stronger. With each step he takes, I can tell he finds it more difficult to walk.

Thoughts come into my head of how to eradicate those invisible germs and cure George of his suffering. *Why can't he take the bandage off? Wouldn't the natural air help heal the infection?* When I have a sore, I lick it to help it heal. *Would George allow me to lick his foot better?*

Days and weeks pass one at a time. There is no visit from George. *Where is he? Have I done anything wrong? How can I communicate to George?*

I wander around my home and stop in front of George's favourite spot, the blue lounge. I discover his scent much stronger here than any other part of our house. I stop and sit here for a while.

—*George I hope you can hear me. I haven't seen you for such a long time and I miss you. It is your right foot isn't it? What's wrong George? What can I do to help you get better? When will I see you again?*

The next day arrives and Mother is all dressed up smartly, wearing blue slacks and a pink cotton jumper. We both go outside in the back yard.

'Teida, I have been asked to do some clerical work at a local firm for a few months starting today, so I need to leave early. I know you are terribly worried about George. I am too. You have been such a good girl. Here is a big bone for you.'

—*Thanks Mother, but I am not hungry. Maybe I will eat it later.*

'I have to go now. I'll see you tonight when I come home.'

As Mother goes to work each day, I pace up and down the yard reflecting on the events leading up to the last day I saw George. Now Mother goes out each day early in the morning and comes home at all different times; sometimes early, sometimes late. All our routines are being turned upside down. She looks just as tired as me.

Sensing my anxiety, Millie comes over.

—*Teida I want to tell you something. You haven't been yourself lately, pacing up and down, wondering whether you will see George again. Stay calm Teida, have faith and pray to God. Pray to Him and tell Him all your worries. Annie has been out more because George is in hospital. It is his right foot Teida. The same foot you noticed with the strong pungent smell. George needs Annie's help to recover.*

Before long you will see George too. Even though he is in hospital, his soul hears you when you are talking to him Teida and he knows how much you miss him. You are comforting him more than you know. George misses you too. Keep talking to him Teida. Tell him more of your comforting thoughts and ideas and about what you get up to during the day. Before too long George will be back to his old antics, playing with you again soon.

—*Millie what is faith and who is God?*

—*Teida, faith is something one hangs on to when there is despair or worry. Faith is that little voice in your head that tells you not to give up, to believe, have hope and stay positive. Faith tells you that everything will be all right in the end. When I was living I prayed every day to God. I released all my worries and concerns to Him, knowing He is the one that will take care of everything for me. God is the divine power from above who is looking after Annie and George right now.*

Taking Millie's advice, I talk to God.

—*God, my name is Teida. I haven't spoken to you like this before. My best friend George is very sick. He is in a lot of pain. He has a very sore leg and I miss him. Millie said for me to talk to you as I worry about George. Will I see him again? Are you the one that will make him better so he can run around and play ball with me once more? And can you look after Mother too? She is so tired and worn out these days.*

The next morning, not being a work day, Mother stays home. Picking up the receiver of the ringing telephone, brimming excitement overflows from Mother's voice. I stay nearby, looking at her with curiosity.

—*Who is that, Mother? It's George isn't it? Please let me say hello*, I say, putting my paw up and trying to grab the telephone off her.

'Yes Teida, you are right, I am speaking to George. Hang on George; there is someone here who wants to say hello. She misses you terribly.'

When she lowers the phone to my ears I hear a familiar voice from the other side. One I have been attuned to for a long time.

Breathing and licking into the phone I say hello to my long lost friend. At the same time, my head turns from side to side hoping he may be close by, on his way to visit me. *Where is he? Why can't I see him?* The conversation ends.

Mother opens the front door. Fresh air blows inside. With bated breath I stand by in anticipation. My eyes dart left and right in search for George. Perhaps George is outside wanting to come in. After a while, I realize George isn't coming over today.

More days and nights pass, one after the other. Another weekend is now upon us. 'Teida, I have to go out for a while. When I come home, I'll have a surprise for you. I won't be long.'

Hmmm! I wonder what Mother has planned?

Out of the blue, I am drawn to a familiar sound coming from the driveway. One I have been looking so much forward to hearing. With the breeze blowing, something catches my eye. Mother opens the back door and lets me inside. Instantly I bolt to the front door. *I know I just heard George's car. How can George's car be in our driveway without George? He is the one who drives his car. Where is he?*

'Teida, are you ready for your surprise? Wait here with me.'

Holding the door open, Mother patiently waits with me by her side. Climbing one step at a time, I finally catch the sight of someone else entering our home. George! After a month or two, he has finally returned.

Jumping up and down, smiling and wagging my tail I make a mad dash towards him, wanting to celebrate.

—*Where have you been George? I am so happy to see you!*

I suddenly realize that the bad smell is gone. No matter how much I keep sniffing around George, there is no smell. It seems to have vanished into thin air. Talk about extremes. First a bad smell and now no smell, what happened? And there is no motley color on his right foot either. Lifting my head up and down, checking George out from top to bottom, he looks the same. Yet something seems to be different.

Plonking on his favourite lounge, he takes off his shoes and socks, allowing his feet to breathe. Unfastening something near his knee at the edge of his shorts, something strange catches my eye. *Am I seeing things?* George now has only one full leg and foot, and half a leg with no foot. Why? The right lower leg and foot is missing. No wonder there isn't any smell.

George explains in more detail the whole story, as I sit attentively, both ears capturing every word. I learn that George had to go to hospital for a big operation. His right leg had to be amputated below the knee. George's diabetes had worsened. The circulation wasn't getting down to the wound on the heel of his right foot. It became infected and gangrenous, causing the bad smell to his right foot. That same odour I used to smell around George.

—*Poor George, no wonder you were in lots of pain.*

Fitting onto George's knee is a scentless prosthetic leg that enables George to walk on two legs. As I bump into it, resting against the lounge, I find the prosthetic leg is much more durable, feels more rubbery and strong. It seems to be the same texture as one of my kong toys outside. The prosthetic leg isn't soft, like a normal leg.

Now he is back there is no way I am going to take my eyes off him, remaining ever vigilant. *Phew! What a relief George didn't go away forever.* I am so happy now that we can see each other again. Millie was right. I prayed to God and now George is here. *Thank you God for making George better and having him see me again.* Miracles do happen, don't they!?

'Hey move away, that's my chair. I'm back now,' says George to me, jokingly, pushing me out of the way from where I am trying to sit on the floor in front of his blue lounge. He sits down and removes his prosthetic leg, making himself more at home. There is not much room for the two of us, so I move aside and keep watch.

'You know George, Teida sat here all the time when you were in hospital,' Mother tells George. 'She either sits here or on her mat in the corner.'

George now realizes he has competition. Of course that is me. So we start playing a new game called musical chairs, without the music. I let George win, knowing that when he goes home it is my turn to sit in front of his favourite chair.

George is visiting regularly again and I am always nearby giving him plenty of licks and cuddles. There is one thing though. I do have to be careful when jumping off after my cuddles. Sometimes I hit George with my paws in an uncomfortable place. Whoops! A dog at times is not always dainty or ladylike. I am not anyway.

ADVICE FROM THE ANIMAL FRIENDS

Sitting on the arm of his favourite lounge. Croakiness in his voice as he struggles to speak softly, trying to breathe at the same time. His neck swollen. His throat sore.

Crumbs of his custard tart fall on the floor and I clean them up, remaining vigilant.

Physically exhausted, lying down on the spare bed, dozing off, waking up an hour or two later. Now there are irregular short visits. I know this isn't like George.

Unfortunately, being a dog, I am unable to call George and check how he is. I leave this all up to Mother. I only see George when he is well enough to visit.

Watching Mother tirelessly at the computer day and night, tapping her fingers on the keyboard, the radio on in the background, I sit nearby. 'What am I looking for? I'm not giving up. There has to be a way to help George, but what? I just don't know what to do. Teida, I am so tired.'

Mother collapses on the floor and starts crying. I walk up to her.

—*Mother, don't worry, we can make George better. What about if we pray? Maybe God can help.* I walk up to her and give her a lick. She doesn't move. I realize that she has cried herself to sleep. I sit and ponder.

What can a dog do? Who can I ask? George is seriously sick, and all Mother and I want is to have him better again. Perhaps Mrs Spider, Mr Worm or my other animal friends know something. Then maybe, as Millie says, God can help. I'll pray to him too.

Maybe what cures animals could cure humans? If humans use a phone or mail to contact each other, how can I contact my dog siblings who perhaps are still living?

Another work day arrives and Mother lets me outside. I see Mr Ant traveling along the crevices of the pathway.

—*Hello Teida.*

—*Hello Mr Ant, do you mind if I ask you for some advice? George is very sick. What can I do to help him get better?*

—*Well Teida, I didn't want to interfere, but recently I have noticed George hasn't been himself. He looks pale and withdrawn. There seems to be much on his mind. When you haven't been yourself, Mother gives you a cuddle. She lies down on the floor next to you and snuggles right up to you. Is there a way you can do that to George? He needs extra support without too much being said. Someone to be there for comfort, giving him lots of love. I know how much you love George, Teida.*

—That's a good idea, Mr Ant. I'll snuggle and stay extra close to George when he lies down on the bed.

I frolick in the garden for a while, taking in the smell of the fresh air and taking on board all the advice Mr Ant has given me. Humans seem to look to medicines for a cure. Everything seems to get complicated. Simplicity just may be the answer. George loves playing ball and hanging out, with me. Maybe I can give him extra licks and cuddles.

'Teida! Hi Teida!'

—Hi Mother, you're home early. Is everything all right? You look so tired.

'Teida, after such a late night yesterday, I can hardly keep my eyes open. I came home early from work so I can have an early night. I am going off to bed now. Good night Teida, I'll see you in the morning.'

Overtiredness sets in as I try to go off to sleep too. Instead, tossing and turning, my inner thoughts swirl around in my head. Seconds pass, then minutes. Empty, quiet minutes, one following the other. Eventually, morning breaks.

Being on call all day and all night; Mother frequently goes out at all odd times with me outside more and more. Today, bumping into Mr Ant, I give him an update while Mother is out seeing George.

—Hi Teida, how did the suggestions go? asks Mr Ant.

—I haven't seen George since we spoke, Mr Ant.

Mrs Spider comes over and offers her suggestions.

—Is there a way you can visit George? Will Mother take you next time she goes to see him? asks Mrs Spider.

—Keep talking to him Teida. His inner soul knows you talk to

him and how much you worry and care about him, Mr Worm joins in the conversation.

Sally Snail also has a recommendation.

—*Teida, do you know many of the plants in your garden have healing properties? The lavender is very calming, the lemon and mandarin trees are very uplifting. Some plants have antiseptic properties. Then there are the roses. Each plant has something special and unique to offer. Next time George visits, have him come out here in your backyard. Get him to inhale the scent of a lemon tree, rub his fingers against the leaves and absorb the fresh fragrance of the roses. I believe this will help his recovery.*

Sally thinks for a moment, looking concerned about something.

Annie looks so tired now. Is there a way you can help her more? she asks. *She needs a lot of strength to help George get through all this.*

—*I worry about Mother too. She raises her voice a lot more and becomes angry. Then she starts crying. What can I do to help her? It upsets me to see her this way.*

Pruning the roses in the rose garden, Millie comes over and joins in the conversation.

—*Teida there is a lot going on with Annie working and helping George during the day and night. By the time she comes home she is so worn out and like you does not sleep much. When humans have a lot on their mind, they are sensitive to everything around them. Annie has been finding it difficult to talk about things so she turns to you. Just be there for her. She is so thankful that you are there for her. Keep praying and believing. Never give up hope.*

Like Mr Worm says, talking to George is good for his soul.

Share with George all the good times you have had together, the fun times, how you play ball together, how he makes you laugh. He needs to have a smile on his face and stay positive. His mind needs to be strong to get through his sickness. Share with George all the memories you have and how much you want to see him again. Ask his soul what it needs so George can get better again. Keep talking to him Teida.

FINAL MOMENTS

A few days after receiving words of advice from my animal friends, something unexpected happens. On Saturday morning, Mother arrives home from shopping after being out for longer than normal.

'Hello Teida, I know I have been out a bit longer this morning. I have a surprise for you.' Following Mother, I notice she is not the only one inside our home. Seeing George, I'm totally in shock.

—*What's happened?* He looks terrible, worse than I have ever seen him before. Sunken eyes, low energy, a gloomy aura in our presence. George's demeanour is altered. Intuitively sensing George's condition declining further, I discover there is something terribly wrong. A dull grayness that tastes like nothing and smells like nothing. It is as if you can reach into the air for miles on end and not touch a single object in front of you. Everything looks different. It is as if dull paint has been splattered into the atmosphere, covering everyone and everything in sight. George's vibration seems to be lifting to another world. I can see his body, but maybe his spirit has partially left his body. He has a vague and blank look on his face.

Frail and slow, this once strong and solid man standing in front of me still manages to smile, radiating peace and love on his face. An expression I can only describe as a smile from heaven. Pride runs through me as I take in his face. Feeling stillness and silence creeping up, without a second thought, instead of running around and showing excitement I become slow and gentle, staying closer and not leaving his side. Standing up to this distasteful energy, hoping like a super hero I can keep it away from my friend George. Putting my detective cap on is now crucial, I must investigate and figure out what is happening.

Will today be the last time I see George? Stop thinking such horrible thoughts. That will never happen. Not if I can help it. Not to my friend George.

Teetering over kissing and patting me on the forehead, with a voice so husky and deep that it is almost impossible to understand he says: 'Teida, I love you. I have missed seeing you. You know I am going to beat this, don't you? Then we can play our games of ball again.'

George does remember. I am so glad he is still alive, his mind positive and active, and he's aware of his surroundings. However, his body is physically falling apart. So much anguish, so much pain. Stopping in her tracks, observing from further away, Mother notices my sudden change in behaviour. Animals will never leave a person's side if someone is seriously ill or dying. *Is George dying?* I follow George as he slowly makes his way to the spare bedroom, taking much longer than usual. His legs use so much effort to walk one step at a time. *If I stay next to George, will I be able to keep this grim reaper's cloud away?*

'I'm just going to hang out the washing George. Teida will look after you,' says Mother. George nods his head in acknowledgement. 'Teida, now you stay here and look after George.'

With his eyes closing, immediately George removes his prosthetic leg, placing it on the floor next to him. He lies down on the spare bed, falling asleep straight away. His hand is outstretched below, reaching out, wanting me to take hold and not let go. Licking his hand, I tell George I am by his side. He opens his eyes, looking downward.

'Teida, I have something to tell you that is very important. I need you to pay attention and listen to me very carefully. The reason I am not well is because I have just been diagnosed with cancer and things do not look good. Once I see the specialist next week, I will know more. There will be many more ups and downs. It isn't that I am afraid of dying, I am just not ready to go. I have too many things that I still need to finish. I am going to stay strong and not let this beat me. I am going to get well again, but it will take a lot of time, so you just have to bear with me. I love you Teida. I love your Mother too.'

I know George is sick but what he just told me sounds life-threatening. *Is cancer the distasteful energy I am sensing around George? What is cancer? Can dogs get cancer too?*

George takes a breath and coughs before he continues talking. 'Annie is one of my best friends Teida. She inspires me. She is so patient and kind. We understand each other, and at the drop of a hat, when I need someone, she is always there. I am so grateful for having both of you in my life Teida. I don't know where I would be today without the two of you.'

George stops talking. He briefly catches a glimpse of me before closing his eyes again. He has never told me anything like that before.

Suddenly George's breathing pattern changes. His breaths become more deliberate, slower and slower, deeper and deeper, as he inhales and exhales one breath at a time. Some loud, some soft. Then for a millisecond he stops, an eternity that makes me wonder if I have witnessed his last breath, before George starts breathing normally again. There is total stillness. Not a twitch or a spasm as he lies snuggled up on the bed, totally motionless. He starts snoring. I realize George is now fast asleep. Peace and serenity fill the room. Perhaps total relaxation and tranquillity is what George needs to get better. Something as simple as a good sleep and having his loyal dog friend stay by his side.

Staying next to George, I think about what Mr Ant suggested; that I snuggle up by his side. Similar to what Mother does when I need someone. With George sound asleep I would rather not disturb him, so I decide to just remain in vigil on the floor.

Awaking what seems to be a long time afterwards, George stretches his arms and legs. Using every ounce of energy and strength he can muster he peels himself off the bed. I move to the side, enabling George to put his foot on the ground and balance himself so he can sit up. 'Have you been here all this time?' George asks me.

I wag my tail and look up into George's soulful eyes, watching him as he puts on his prosthetic leg. I can tell George is more rested and a lot calmer. He enjoyed coming over. It was good we were able to spend one on one time together, and at the same time, I was able to watch over him. Hopefully, it won't be so long before we catch up again. Hopefully he quickly recovers.

Mother enters the room. 'Teida, I am going to take George home now. I'll be about twenty minutes.'

—*Mother, before George goes home, can he walk along the garden first? There are plenty of plants in our garden with healing properties that will help him get better, and what about a game of ball? George loves stirring me up when he plays ball.*

'Goodbye Teida, I'll see you soon. I feel so much better after my afternoon nap. A weight has lifted off my shoulders. I have much more energy now. Teida, your love and compassion really helped me sleep this afternoon. Better than any medicine a doctor or nurse can give. You gave me tranquillity and peace. I haven't had a good sleep in such a long time. I can now deal with the cancer and the pain. Coming here and being with you is just what the doctor ordered. Don't worry; I will be back. I won't make it so long next time. Remember what I just told you, I am not going to let this beat me. I have to get worse before I get better.'

As Mother, George and I leave the bedroom we stop. 'I want to sit outside in the backyard for a minute,' says George. 'I want to inhale the fresh air, walk along the garden. It has been a while since I have been out here.' I follow them out.

—*Go this way George. Look at the citrus trees, touch the leaves, and crush some lavender between your fingers.*

'There is nothing like the smell of nature, is there?' says George, as we walk past the rose garden and citrus trees. He squeezes some lavender between his fingers and the aroma of the flowers wafts by with the passing wind.

'Here George, have a passionfruit,' Mother says, as she picks a ripe passionfruit off the vine overhanging the garden shed.

'That tastes so sweet. So different to the passionfruit you buy,' remarks George.

We all step up onto the back deck. Suddenly, a ball drops in front of George's feet. I sit in anticipation.

'All right Teida, let's have a small game,' George says as he bends over to pick up the ball. 'Here you go girl. Go get the ball.'

Prancing back I swing the ball from side to side. Then I bash the ball on the grass before hurling it into the air once more. Then, thud! The ball drops at George's feet, waiting for his next move.

Bending over and picking up the white, squashed, medium size ball, George throws it. Deep in concentration, I turn my head left and right and look all around. Lowering my snout, my paws ready, I am preparing to run and defend my surrounding area as I play goal keeper. Suddenly, I stop dead in my tracks. I didn't see the ball go past.

—*Where did it go? Did you really toss the ball for me to chase? What have you done with the ball? Woof! Woof!*

Patiently I stare at George and wait in anticipation. He is trying to play tricks, with a smile from ear to ear. Finally George retrieves the ball from behind his back, hurling it across the yard. There is no way he can fool such a clever dog as me. He takes a deep breath and stops, unable to bend over to pick up the ball. I sense he has to go home and lie down.

Watching and listening is something I always do. Hearing people talk, I listen. Hearing words they are not saying, the words they want to say, and the words they keep inside their heart. Sharing in their joy, their happiness, and their pain. Seeing George I know. There is frustration and hurt. He is holding his composure, trying to win this latest battle, not allowing this illness to defeat him.

'Goodbye old girl. Be strong. I'll be back. You wait and see.' Mother takes George home after his stroll along the garden.

Why George? I am not able to bring myself to say goodbye. I don't want him to die. Perhaps my instincts are wrong. This is the first time I have ever experienced this type of connection with a human. *What do I do? Who can I ask? Who can I turn to and question my feelings and intuition?* I need to get answers urgently! Really fast! With George's power and mind I am sure he can beat this illness and pain. He is always so positive.

I don't want to separate from George. Nobody does. We are bonded together as dog and man. As long as I am around I will do my best to make sure George stays alive. We will always be together; never alone and without companionship.

George is a fighter and has fought off other battles before, physical and mental, every disease, illness or whatever comes across him. I see a twinkle in his eye telling me he is here to the end. George likes to do things his way. He never likes anyone mothering him. Mother and I have to be patient and support him in any way we can. Even if it is just being there, close by his side.

Why is there no remedy to cure his illnesses? What is happening to George and why? He is such a good person. A special man, always there, who does anything for anyone. He doesn't deserve to be suffering. He deserves better. Why is his health suddenly spiralling downwards? Instinctively I am aware that there are two conversations going on in George's head. Subconsciously, George knows his time is coming to an end. However, consciously, George isn't ready to die, not yet. As George said to me, he has still so much to accomplish. I have to be positive; positive for Mother and especially for George.

Mother comes home after dropping George home to his place. I look up at her with my questions.

Mother, what is happening to George? Despondently, her eyes tell me things have worsened. She doesn't know why. About a week after George's visit, George is admitted to hospital.

CHAPTER 16

VISITING GEORGE

'Teida, I have just come back from the hospital. I didn't stay long as George was tired. He had many people visit him earlier in the day. Since I am not working tomorrow, how about we go see George?'

—Me, visit George? That's a good idea. Something to cheer him up, lift his spirits, motivate him to keep going.

Since George is too sick to visit and play with me, it is my turn this time, and I am looking forward to seeing my friend and giving him cuddles. Of course, I will have to be on my best behaviour. I need to be gentle. Is a human hospital the same as an animal hospital?

Mother secures me in the car and off we go. We drive along a busy road and stop at the traffic lights as they change from green to red. Then after a short time, we continue on our journey as the traffic lights change back to green again. I spot ambulances and emergency transport vehicles and realize we have arrived at the hospital.

Mother helps me out of the car and together we walk across the road to a big building with a sign saying Hospital Health Care. That must be the place. Through the automatic doors I see a large foyer area with square rugs and seating.

We walk over to the reception desk.

'Hello, are you able to tell me what room George is in?' asks Mother.

'You're here to see George? I was told to be expecting you today,' said the receptionist. 'George is on the first floor. Once you get out of the lift walk straight down to the end. You will see him in the corner room on the left. He is looking forward to seeing you. How about I take you? It is very unusual to have a dog visit a patient here.'

'Thank you so much for your help,' replies Mother.

As we walk to the lift, people pass by, looking puzzled.

'I didn't think dogs are allowed here,' I hear someone say gruffly. 'I wasn't allowed to bring my dog,' says another.

We all get into the lift and go up to the next floor.

After stepping out, I start sniffing around trying to find George's scent. There are only human smells here, no animal smells. *Why are there not other animals visiting?*

'I'll leave you here. George is down there, the last room on the left,' the nurse tells Mother. 'Thank you so much. You have been very helpful. Have a good day,' says Mother.

—*This hallway is a good area to play ball, isn't it Mother? When George is well enough maybe we can bring one of my balls and roll it up and down.*

Walking into George's room there is an overpowering smell of disinfectant. I sense the confusion, uncertainty and helplessness of the many sick people clinging onto life in the hope of being home again soon. *Will George make it home?*

Plain white walls and plastic trim surround me from all angles, with the exception of the cold metal door allowing you in and out. Puffy white pillows support George as he props himself to sit up, nothing like the bed at home. The hospital bed being so much higher, I wonder if George's hand can reach down and pat me. Inserted into George's right wrist is a needle attached to a plastic bag with liquid hanging from a steel pole with wheels next to him. He reaches down to pat me. Mother finds a chair beside George's bed to sit on.

'Hi George,' Mother says. 'How did you sleep last night? Are the needles giving you trouble?'

George smiles, 'Hello, it is good to see you Teida. Hello Annie. I had a bad night last night.'

He tells us that the intravenous drip on his right arm is to give him liquids and rehydrate him so he gets enough nutrition throughout the day. The one of the left is for medicine and pain killers.

'It looks painful but doesn't hurt too much.'

George takes a breath and continues. 'Teida, I am so glad you made it here. I have to stay in hospital until I get better. I cannot do very much but rest and watch television. People come and visit when they can, then I get tired and go to sleep. A nurse comes every four hours to monitor my sugar levels, check my blood pressure and adjust the medicine.'

A lady wearing a blue uniform comes to the entrance of the door. She speaks differently than George and Mother, her voice very precise and clipped.

'Hello George, I have come to check on you before you have your dinner. Oh! You have visitors. This must be the dog everyone has been talking about,' the nurse says as she enters the room.

I look at the nurse and wag my tail.

After checking George's sugar levels and blood pressure the nurse speaks to George. 'Your blood pressure is fine. I will return with your insulin shortly. Dinner will be served in about 30 minutes.'

'Thanks love,' says George.

How is George going to get better in here? No playing ball, no favourite blue lounge to sit on. No bright colors on the walls to cheer him up.

'What is it like outside?' George asks Mother. 'I'm getting a bit cold. The air conditioner isn't working too well today.'

'It has been a lovely sunny day today. Not much wind. Now it is getting a bit cloudy.'

How can a hospital be a place of healing when all someone does is come in, give you medicine, check on your health and go away?

George presses the buzzer and another nurse enters the ward. 'The drip is beeping,' George tells the nurse. The nurse takes a look, replaces the plastic bag with more rehydrating liquid before hurriedly walking away to the sound of someone else's buzzer going off in the background. She looks sad and run off her feet.

'I'm getting a bit tired now. I have to wait for my dinner and then I will have an early night and go off to sleep,' says George.

—*George, can I stay here with you?* I ask, looking up at George with beckoning eyes. Mother pulls on the leash, wanting me to move forward.

'Teida, the nurse gave me permission for you to come for short visits. I'm sorry, I'm no fun today,' George says, leaning over and giving me a pat. 'Talk to me like you do, through your mind to mine. Come and visit with Annie again soon. Remember, I am going to beat this, and before too long I will be home playing ball again.'

'Teida, George isn't going anywhere. He needs to have his dinner now, and we need to go home and have our dinner too. Don't worry we will come back and visit George again.'

CHAPTER 17

DEATH AND DYING

Waiting outside for Mother to come home from work, taking in the scented fragrance of the night air, I cannot help but feel a sense of devastating and profound loss. *Has someone died? No, it couldn't be Mother or George, could it?* I only saw George the other day and even though he was tired he seemed to be in good spirits. Something just tells me, but what, I am not sure. My heart just feels totally empty.

Looking above to the dark blackened skies, illuminated by the glittering stars silhouetted against the silvery moon. Soft, shimmering pathways of shadows are created throughout the garden. Gazing around I notice my brush, basketball, my balls large and small, as well as my frisbee scattered on the grass. Patiently I wait and wait. *Why is Mother so late coming home? Has something happened to her?*

Sniffing up and down the yard, I investigate each blade of grass, no pebble left unturned. There is total quiet, seeming louder than the noise of the routines of the day. On my own, in the dead of night, restless, unable to settle down, I wait and wait in the hope Mother will return home soon. The air remains calm and silent. No familiar sounds. No familiar words. Even the telephone inside is silent. I stay close to the back door and hope it won't be long until I am let inside.

In the seconds following, which seem like hours, a vision appears in front of me. I sit hypnotized, staring and watching as it slowly reveals itself. The vision is a small golden halo, being carried by many angels. It is all very beautiful. As the vision comes closer, the angels release the golden halo into the air and step into the background. The golden halo increases in size, becoming bigger and bigger. Gradually emerging from the golden halo another image appears. Someone I recognize, now so tall and strong, upright and proud, so glorious and whole, vibrantly illuminated, free of suffering and with a beaming, loving smile. *No, it couldn't be; could it? Am I seeing who I think I am seeing?*

—*All will be fine Teida, make sure you look after Annie.*

Now I understand what the devastating loss is all about. *Does Mother know? How do I tell her?* She will be so upset, so lost.

Stunned, I sit on the soft lawn, motionless, taking it all in. Every word, every vision; trying to make sense of what has just occurred, absorbing the amazing experience. Realizing I have been privileged that George came to say goodbye.

There is so much to think about. *Did George really know he was dying? How did he know it was his time? I wonder how* he arrived in heaven. *Did he know where heaven is? Was there anyone to meet him? What type of place is heaven?* Something like this has never happened to me before.

Millie pops over.

—*Teida, I have something very important to explain to you.*

I follow her shining light and we sit together on the edge of the back deck, looking out into the garden in front of us. I look straight into Millie's eyes, listening to every word.

—*Teida, we are all very shocked and sad about George. You knew it was very serious the last time he was over. I want you to realize your instincts were right. Teida, we knew too. You see Teida, we all come on earth to learn lessons and teach others life lessons. Life is a school for our soul to learn and, once it is time, we all go back to heaven. It was George's time to go home. This life lesson, you had to learn for yourself, so no one was able to tell you ahead of time.*

—*Millie, does Mother know?*

—*Annie does know. She was about to leave work and the telephone rang. Her boss answered the call and by the tone of her voice Annie realized what the phone call was about. Throughout the day she instinctively felt things were not right with George. She was told not to make contact with George and George never called her like he usually does. Her intuition was telling her the end of the life for George was near. Her emotions have been up and down like a roller coaster.*

I hear Mother's car pulling into the driveway as Millie continues.

—*Annie is very fragile Teida. Teida, you and Annie will learn how to communicate more with the spirit world. Both your lives will start a new journey; much better for you and much better for Annie. George and I will be guiding you as well as all your spirit guides, angels and fairies. We will all be around you, comforting you during this difficult time. Annie needs you Teida. Remember what George said, make sure you look after Annie, it is really important.*

—I will Millie, thank you for being with me.

Millie disappears and the sensor light shines from the front yard. I hear someone fumble for the keys at the front door. The front door unlocks. Mother has finally come home from her long day at work. In seconds I will see her. Mother lets me inside. Thinking back to the conversation I had with Millie, looking at Mother I can see she knows the devastating news about George.

As mum looks down at me, I notice color dissipating from her face as if a ghost is in sight. Her eyes are bloodshot and saturated, red from all the tears which have fallen down the side of her face. I have never seen her so emotionally traumatized. Unlike a tap where you can turn it off and on, Mother sobs uncontrollably, unable to stop.

Tossing her bags then walking down the hallway, Mother finally stops at her bedroom. I wait for her outside. She comes out again, her clothes loose and comfortable now.

Upon reaching the lounge room, our silence is broken by the ringing of the telephone. 'Who could that be?' As Mother reaches for the white cordless phone, the telephone stops ringing. 'Damn, I missed that call; they'll call later.'

She grabs the cordless phone and puts it on the glass coffee table before plonking herself in one big flop down to my level on the floor. 'Teida, I have bad news I need to tell you,' Mother talks, her voice stuttering, trying to put her sentence together. 'George has died. He died early this evening. That is why I was home late tonight. We won't be going to see him at the hospital anymore. Stay with me Teida; I need to make some phone calls.'

Mother picks up the cordless phone and starts dialling.

'Dad, I've just come home. Did you call earlier? I picked up the phone and no one was there.'

Mother's dad replies, and she shakes her head.

'I'll be okay, Dad. There's no need to come over. I'm going to sleep now. Love you Dad. Speak to you tomorrow.'

Mother hangs up.

One phone call over with, I can imagine there are many more to come. This time the phone rings.

'Hello Mother. I just came home from work.'

'It will be great to see you on the weekend. Thank you. I could do with some company. I'm going to bed now. See you.'

She lifts my paws gently onto her lap and, with Mother on the floor next to me, we sit quietly. The telephone has stopped ringing. No more phone calls for tonight. I peer deeply into Mother's melancholy dark brown eyes with commiseration and understanding. We reflect, trying to piece together all of today's events.

Mother puts her arms around me, clinging tightly. Lowering her head, waves of sorrow drench my fur. Like a towel, my fur helps dry Mother's face.

Out of control, our hearts spiral into a deep abyss, shattering the warmth and confidence from within. Walking around slower than usual, yawning, not knowing what to do next.

Maybe it is all a dream. Maybe it isn't real. It could be my imagination.

I know it isn't. I knew the last time George visited something wasn't right. I just didn't want to accept that last visit from George to our home would be so final. Deep down his fight for life has now come to a close.

From the various conversations Mother has had since George's death, I learn that George died shortly after being admitted to hospital, nearly two weeks after he visited our home for what turned out to be the last time. At least I was given the opportunity to visit George in hospital. Separating from someone you really love and care about is the hardest thing to do. There was no desire to go our own different ways. *Why couldn't we all go together?* I guess this is why dogs fret so much for their owner when their owner passes before them.

Why was I unable to express my thoughts and feelings to Mother beforehand? Why couldn't I prepare Mother? Did she know herself? Was I able to have done anything different? More licks, more nudges, more playing ball. Will I be able to talk to George in heaven? So many questions were going through my head.

Feeling incredibly sad, deep down I know it is for the best that George died fairly quickly and in minimal pain. The less he suffered the better. From my observations, he did have a hard life here on earth and going to heaven will be a whole new better world of peace and happiness for him. No sickness. No suffering. Free from his ravaged body, happily reuniting with the family members who passed before him in the other world, on the other side. It is hard for everyone, the people and animals left behind, yet I know George is in a far better place than we can even imagine.

CHAPTER 18

FAREWELL GEORGE

Waking up before dawn and finding Mother still sleeping, I mosey out to the living room and sit in front of George's favourite blue lounge. I gaze at the many items surrounding me: the daily newspapers thrown on the floor next to the coffee table, hiding my shedding fur; the two large royal blue cushions that have fallen off the lounge during the night; Mother's black handbag hanging off the back of the chair … and the many photos displayed of George in happier times. Then it hits me.

What about Mother? Will she go too and leave me all on my own? How will I handle facing the whole world alone? I hope Mother stays with me forever. I don't want her to leave too.

After the news of George's death, I stay more and more by Mother's side, remaining vigilant. I watch Mother as she gives her tireless fingers a work out, instinctively dialling and contacting every person possible and informing them of the sad news, one person after another. Mother does not want people to know later. She wants them to know now, immediately providing them with the opportunity to say goodbye. Whoever she can think of, she calls, with a tone of reassurance and compassion in her voice.

All these people are shocked over the unexpected news. I mean, who wouldn't be? George left a lasting impression on everyone he met. From her conversations, I hear her discuss the upcoming funeral and all the preparations that need to take place. Mother has been asked to carry George's medals in the funeral procession. I am very proud of Mother. It appears not many people ever understood the close bond we all had – George, Mother and me.

The day of the funeral finally arrives. Mother is all dressed up, wearing her official uniform for the emergency service: a pale blue, short sleeve blouse with her medals pinned on and epaulettes down the shoulders, and gray trousers. Her black shoes are so shiny they mirror my reflection. Turning to Mother, I see her mouth is smiling yet her eyes tell another story; showing her despair and sadness. She is afraid. She is alone.

'Teida I wish you could come too. Unfortunately, dogs are not allowed, only humans. I'll be all right. I have no idea how to get to the venue so I need to leave early just in case I get lost, and you know what I am like parking the car. Bye Teida. I'll see you when I come home. I am unsure how long I will be. Look after the house. I love you.'

After saying goodbye and giving me a big hug, Mother puts me outside and leaves. Driving somewhere she has never been before; she knows she has to be strong and do this for George. I have total faith in Mother. Her family will be at the funeral service waiting to support her.

With Mother away, what am I to do now? Looking around I see my friends Mr Worm, Mr Ant, and Sally Snail all coming towards me.

Pacing up and down the side fence, checking out the cars as they drive by, I hope one may slow down to a halt and park in the driveway. *Is anybody stopping? Is anyone coming over to say hello? Who will give me surprise visits when I am on my own?*

—Hi Teida, sounds a voice from above. Looking up, I see Mrs Spider hanging from her web.

—*We all have come over to keep you company while Annie is away. It won't be the same without George, will it? We miss him too. We noticed how you both had so much fun playing together and being with each other. Remember the good times Teida. Remember all the fun times you had together.*

I am so thankful to see Mrs Spider, Mr Worm and Mr Ant, with my feeling of emptiness inside; all lost and alone. Not long after Millie visits, bringing with her many bouquets of beautiful, brightly colored roses, large and small. She describes to me George's funeral service.

—*Teida, Annie is doing well. Her dad, sister and uncle are all with her. She proudly carried George's medals down the aisle during the funeral service. There were so many people, many even standing outside the small chapel. With the service now finished, Annie is now at the emergency service organisation having something to eat and drink. There are camel rides in memory of George and yes; even though Annie has a fear of heights, she bravely rode a camel too, with the support of another lady who held her from behind. George loved camels Teida. He had a big collection of camel memorabilia. Annie will be home soon Teida. She is shattered, very drained and looking forward to being home again. George is very proud of both of you today.*

—*Millie, why are funerals only for humans?*

—*Teida, each person and their family choose the funeral they would like to have. Annie would have taken you if she was able.*

Millie continues to talk and cheer me up.

—*Teida, have a look at the pink blossoms showing their small, delicate, bright pink petals against the burgundy leaves. George planted this shrub and it is blooming so beautifully. Over the other side, can you see the posies of small white and yellow daisies? Throughout the yard the magnificent flowers are displaying bright, uplifting colors; all to cheer you up.*

Up in the nearby trees, I see many vibrations of colorful wings flapping like hummingbirds. Neighboring butterflies come over to bring cheerful messages of compassion and love from all the angels and fairies.

—*Teida we understand you miss George terribly. Please do not be upset, we are here for you. George isn't too far away. If you look up at the brightest star glowing at night or the most radiant beam of sunlight during the day you will see him. Sitting inside on the floor in front of George's favourite lounge, you will feel him touch you. Be still and quiet Teida and you will even hear him talk to you. We just want you to know Teida, you will carry his scent with you everywhere you go. That is something only a dog can do. Remember Teida; we are always around to support you.*

After a long day of attending the memorial and funeral service, Mother returns. Totally exhausted, totally drained after a long day. She collapses onto the floor next to me. Instantly I feel her arms cupped around me, holding on, not letting go. My heart is open wide, telling her she is not alone.

CHAPTER 19

COMFORT AND SUPPORT

Sleepless nights, early mornings; the days and nights are the same. I wonder why more time hasn't passed by. Our lives have been hit by a brick wall. Waking up in the middle of the night I hear unfamiliar noises. It sounds like drizzly rain. Investigating, I find Mother sobbing in her sleep, soaking her pillow. I wait despairingly nearby, at the bedroom door. Eventually, she wanders out long enough for me to see her, then goes back to bed again. I rush over and at the same time Mother kneels down in front of me. Tenderly I lick the remnants of grief and sadness away. Her eyelashes cling together, glued with tears in between, her face exhausted. Without words, I know it is the build-up of all her emotions inside. Nothing unnerves me more than watching people I love and care about fall apart. The world makes no sense.

Reminiscing back to the many times George and I had together, I now become aware there will be no more playing ball. No more treats. No more visits or hearing the sound of his voice. No more pats or cuddles. No more trips to the vet in George's car. No more food crumbs or hot chips falling on the floor from his lap for me to eat; no more sneaking a lick of ice cream. No seeing him sitting on the back deck, sipping a cup of coffee from that much-loved mug of his or guzzling his favourite drink, Pepsi Max, straight from the large bottle in the fridge. His humour, his zest for life, his ability to have fun and make me laugh; the very force that made George who he was has now moved on.

Now there is a big gap. *What am I going to do?* Deep down I know I have to just keep going and strive forward, especially for Mother. George previously said to Mother that we both are strong; stronger than we give ourselves credit for. We have to give each other the strength to get up and get through each day, one day at a time.

Trying to sum up the loss of a friend, there is an awful hollow feeling in the pit of my stomach. Rumbling and churning as my chest tightens, my heart aching. Profound sadness, pressing against my chest, ready to erupt, trying to stop me from breathing. Panting and breathing slowly I try and gain control of this terrible queasy feeling. *How much longer do I have to wait for Mother?* I don't want to wake her up. She needs her sleep after being awake for most of the night.

Oh no! I can't wait any longer and need to go outside. What an awful smell! What do I do? What is Mother going to say? Will she punish me?

Stretching as she comes out from her bedroom, her face says it all.

'Teida what happened? That's not like you. You normally wait until you go outside. Don't tell me you are sick too. Are you all right? I could not cope with losing you too.'

Bravely she scrubs and cleans the mishap, making the area smell nice again. Mother didn't react like I thought she would. Yes, she is upset; it was something else she doesn't need. She is still distraught and now has me to worry about too, watching everything I do.

The telephone rings. 'Hi Dad, what are you up to today? Mother's popping over this morning. Have a good day Dad. I'll speak to you this afternoon.' It is a phone call from Mother's dad. Mother speaks to him every morning and every night.

Annie's Mother pops in for a visit, staying for a while and leaving later in the morning. Out in the backyard, I follow Mother into the garden then back inside again.

A new working week comes upon us. 'Teida, it's time to go outside. I'm off to work now. I'll see you when I get home.'

Mother is going off to work, is she going to return home? If one person goes to heaven, maybe it could happen to two. My two best friends.

I think about how much George and Mother used to hang out together, conversing and supporting each other through thick and thin. *Who can Mother go to now? Who just calls her to check how we both are, to say hello or pop in for a visit?* George is the only real friend Mother had. Someone she confided in, who she shared anything and everything with and who understood her. Now Mother is so lonely, so distant, hardly saying a word. She really needs someone. Filled with emptiness, life just isn't the same anymore.

Day by day I keep hoping George will appear, though I know I won't see him anymore. As cars drive down the street I think, is one of them George's car coming up the driveway? Will he materialize right in front of my eyes once again?

Being a dog, I discovered George and I had so much in common. Like me he was spontaneous, mostly living in the moment, the now – and of course we had fun ways of teasing and joking with each other, particularly when we were playing ball. Always communicating, he shared so much love and was always there to lend a hand. He never took life for granted. We never needed words to communicate, knowing exactly how we felt each time we saw each other.

Like humans, dogs have emotions too. Did you know any traumatic event causes grief? Animals, like humans, have feelings; joy, anger, playfulness, pain, sadness and grief. We deserve all the respect and protection our owners can provide. Depression and grief are different. Grief is marked by distress over the loss of another or, in severe cases, overwhelming separation anxiety. Depression is marked by negative thoughts and feelings about oneself, low self-esteem and low self-worth. Dogs need to feel loved and appreciated to be happy, especially during a time of grieving.

Suddenly the days and nights turn bleak and dark. Everything is now in slow motion, taking forever. It appears time just does not go as fast as it used to. Incredibly time keeps moving forward for everyone else in the world. When will I be able to find an opening of light and brightness? All the joys in my life seem to have disappeared; the birds and their singing, the colorful flowers in Mother's garden, even her trees seem to be extra large in size, wider and higher. *Where is Mrs Spider, Mr Worm or Mr Ant? Who can I talk to when Mother isn't home?*

While Mother is weeding the garden and pruning the citrus trees, I watch the flocks of birds flying high and swooping down in front of me, trying to get my attention. People are walking along outside our home. Suddenly a ball drops right next to me.

'Teida, how about playing some ball? Go, go get the ball,' Mother says as she throws it in my direction, wanting to play ball with me. Fetching the ball and returning it to Mother, I notice her looking down.

'Teida what's happened to your leg. Have you been licking your leg?' Tucking my leg inwards, Mother gently brings my leg out and has a look. 'Teida, you have a wound here. I have to fix it for you. We do not want it to get any worse, do we?'

Oh! No! I can't hide anything from her, can I? As a form of comfort, I started licking my leg and now it has created a wound. No matter if Mother is out or at home, if it is night or day, without thinking I start licking. It is like when a human bites their fingernails. I just don't know how to stop. You see, dogs normally lick their wounds as a way to heal. My wound is internal. It is a symptom of separation anxiety, worrying whether I will ever see Mother again when she goes out. Eventually, after some time of Mother's persistence and patience, bribing and coaxing, I ease off. The hair starts to grow back. It becomes itchy and irritating and I begin licking, and it all starts over again. When humans hurt themselves, a scab forms, gets itchy and they scratch it before it heals. My leg is similar.

'Teida, come here.' I hear Mother's vulnerability in her voice. 'You've been feeling anxious just like me, haven't you? I need to stop you licking before the wound worsens.'

She takes off my collar; maybe it is bath time? However, on this occasion, Mother doesn't lift me into the bath. She stays down on the floor next to me, threading a large, plastic-y object through my collar. I haven't seen this object before.

'I know you won't like me putting a clear collar over your head, and I can't blame you. It is called an Elizabethan collar and it is used to stop dogs licking their wounds. We need to get your leg fixed. It is only temporary, until your leg heals.'

Now my head feels heavier. Looking around in every direction I see a transparent object following me here, there and everywhere. I am no longer able to reach my leg.

Following Mother along the hallway, feeling totally unbalanced, I bump into the dining chairs as I go from one room to the next. *Has Mother rearranged the furniture?* The vast open space appears to be much smaller. Narrow aisles and spaces; very little room to walk around. At least I can still eat and drink. It seems like forever, every day and every night that the Elizabethan collar stays around my head.

'Teida, let me take a look,' Mother says, after a whole month. 'It seems your leg has healed. Hold on and I will take this large collar off you.' No more licking and no more bucket thing around my head. I can see all around again. My habit is finally broken. Thanks Mother.

It is difficult knowing George died unexpectedly. It seems time really isn't always on our side. It isn't always patient and kind. It doesn't politely wait in the wings. No matter what, though, Mother is here, and we are going through this together; all the ups and downs, each turbulent wave, floating along the calm river, facing whatever comes towards us. We are surviving together. We are strong. We are a family.

CHRISTMAS COUNTDOWN

S ince George's passing Mother and I have become inseparable; being with each other through good times and bad times, happy time and sad times. No matter what, I want Mother to know that she always has me to share her thoughts and I'm always ready to play with her. I want Mother to realize that she has done more for me than she will ever know. Still, I understand that I am a dog and that there are times when Mother needs a human to talk to. I find Mother's dad – who I call Grandpa-Dad – is taking over the role George used to have, speaking to Mother at least daily.

Then, of course there is Christmas. How can I forget about Christmas? Mother and George always enjoyed Christmas, and I love Christmas too.

Today is the first of December. Time to put up all the Christmas decorations. Mother says that there are only twenty-four days till Christmas. George passed away so recently, but Christmas still comes around.

Christmas carols are playing in the background on Mother's stereo. Mother rises from the lounge chair and walks down the hallway into the spare room, where there are many boxes and containers on top of the cupboard and alongside placed one on top of the other. Much too high for a dog to reach. Stretching up on her toes, Mother grabs a box way up on top, a large worn out box, and brings it into the living room.

Eventually, one by one, all the boxes and containers are all spread on the floor. Each one has an assortment of Christmas decorations, tinsel and ornaments that have been collected over a long period of time.

Mother sits down beside me and pauses.

'Teida, is it worth decorating the house this year? I feel so lonely. I am finding it so hard with George not here.'

–Go on Mother, do it for us. I look up at Mother. *Even though George isn't here, he would be totally upset if you didn't do things like you usually do.* Sitting down, Mother opens the rectangular box and takes out the Christmas tree, all ready to be put together.

Assembling the top to the bottom, fanning out the branches, the Christmas tree stands almost as tall as Mother and is placed on the floor next to the kitchen sideboard. Next Mother opens a large container filled with the many trinkets and ornaments to hang onto the tree. She starts adding all her decorations, one by one, on each branch of the tree. Some fun, others purchased because they were beautiful and then others full of lifetime memories handmade by her mother and now handed down.

Before long our Christmas tree is completely decorated with many colorful Christmas balls, jingling Christmas bells, long red beads weaving in out giving the look of tinsel, and Mother's handmade Christmas angel that sits on top. Mind you; I have to be careful not to bump into the Christmas tree when I play ball up and down the hallway, otherwise the smaller ornaments will fall off and roll all over the floor.

Standing up on the arms of the lounge, Mother hangs different colored tinsel across the picture rails in the living and dining room, with many handmade ornaments threaded through one by one. She then places ornaments on the glass table in the dining room and wooden round table in the living room. A Christmas house with flashing lights in colors of blue, red, green, yellow and white is displayed, surrounded by Santa Claus oil burners and candle holders. Large and small snowmen are placed in between.

There is the nativity scene, representing baby Jesus in a manager. Mother places the nativity scene next to her blue lamp on the wooden round table. It takes me back to what George always told Mother. He never bought a nativity scene unless there was a camel, and they were not easy to find. He explained that the three wise men rode on camels to see baby Jesus, giving him gifts of gold, frankincense and myrrh; but in the shops, he hardly saw a nativity scene that had a camel. Then, last year, as a Christmas present, he found the perfect nativity scene to give to Mother – camel and all.

I remember Mother telling George: 'Guess what … there are so many days till Christmas.' George would respond with his favourite quote, 'Bah Humbug!' In their travels George and

Mother even bought a 'Bah Humbug' beanie hat with flashing lights that Mother still has today. Every month Mother always does a countdown, then as the day comes closer it would be weeks, then days, before Christmas is finally here. She opens each window of her advent calendar leading up to the special day.

But now there is one thing missing. Mother is longing to have someone special in her life. Someone she can share with. I see the disappointment and sadness in Mother's eyes not having anyone to visit and share her enthusiastic Christmas spirit. She decorates her home all alone.

The days soon pass.

'Teida, guess what? Santa's coming tonight. Make sure you go to sleep early!'

Waking up at 5am, Mother calls out to me. 'Teida, come here. Santa's come. Let's look and see what he got you.'

Mother places a Christmas stocking filled with doggie biscuits and treats in front of me. 'Teida look, Santa brought you a Christmas stocking – it has a pig's ear, a sheep's ear, dried liver, small dog biscuits – all the yummy treats I know you will like.'

I have a sniff.

– *Yum! Thanks, Mother!*

'Teida, wait here. I want to take a photo.' Click! A flash goes off.

'I'll take another. Ready Teida?' Flash!

Then she makes a telephone call. 'Hello Dad, are you awake? Santa's come. Merry Christmas Dad.'

Sitting close by her side on Christmas morning, one by one Mother carefully unwraps and shows me all the presents sitting under the Christmas tree. She makes another phone call or two before getting dressed and ready for the day ahead.

'Teida I am going to see my family for Christmas. Unfortunately, you have to stay home. I will see you later on this afternoon.'

Searching high and low as Mother goes visiting with her family, I realize there is no George anymore. No George and no new Christmas ball. Unexpectedly, after feeling totally forgotten, I see a new red roped ball sitting in the backyard. Tradition does continue, even with George in spirit.

QUESTIONS AND ANSWERS

Much time has passed since George went to the spirit realm and I miss him each and every day. I always will. George is always on my mind. I think about all the wonderful things we did together, remembering the good times, the fun times and happy times. All the great lessons he taught me. I often wonder what is he is up to now that he is in heaven.

Staying by Mother's side, I follow her outside into the garden. She gets her orange and black pruners and starts cutting back the overgrown branches of the lemon tree. I walk along the lawn, remembering all the fun times George, Mother and I had playing ball together in the backyard. Will George return and visit me now that he is in heaven?

—*Hello Teida.*

That voice sounds like George. It couldn't be George, could it? Where is the voice coming from? I turn my head left and right.

—Teida I am over here, underneath the canopy of the small bright pink flowers.

—Hi George! It really is you! Have you really come to visit me? I am so excited and happy, my tail wagging back and forth.

—Yes Teida, I have come to visit you. Similar to how I did when I was living. I know you miss me and I miss you too. I am sorry I went the way I did, without opening up more to you and Annie, and I am sorry for what my passing has left you. If only I could take that back, I would. I didn't want to accept that I was leaving you. I found it so difficult to say goodbye. To me saying goodbye is so final and something I never came to terms with. You knew more about me than I did myself.

—George, I knew you were afraid. Mother and I never blame you for anything. We were afraid too.

—You have been asking many questions and I hope today I can answer these questions for you. Heaven is a magnificent place Teida, more than anyone can imagine, a place with such freedom and love. When I first arrived I was met by my loved ones; all those who died before me were here to greet me. I reunited with my mother and father, my siblings and all the animals that I had as pets on earth. I have even seen many angels and spirit guides who have supported me along the way.

Teida, I even met your dog Mama, too. She says that you are so loyal, caring and nurturing. She is so proud of you, Teida, and watches over you always. She says that you are just like her with your maternal instincts.

—Are you better George?

—Teida, I am in a good and safe place and free from all my illnesses and pain. Look, I even have my leg back too. I can *run around, dance and even play ball with you again. I can eat anything from ice cream to custard tarts, from sweet foods to savoury foods, without monitoring my sugar anymore. There is no time like day or night, morning or afternoon, late or early.*

—*George, I feel so guilty I couldn't do anything more to help you.*

—*You did so much to help me and I cannot thank you enough. Staying by my side in the final moments when I fell asleep on the bed, being with me and suggesting I have a last walk in the garden, putting my body at rest so I could go to heaven peacefully. All these and everything before were such a help Teida. My time was up, and when it is your time, you will know too.*

—*George, what will happen when I die? Will I go to heaven too? What will happen to Mother? By the time I die I want there to be someone special in her life. She is so lonely.*

—*Teida, heaven is for everyone, for humans, for plants, for animals and even dogs. Every living thing goes to heaven,* George reassures me.

Try and not to think about what will happen when you die. Everything will fall into place. Annie is opening up spiritually. A lot will happen before it is your time. Teida, I am very proud of you. Know I am always here, close by your side, guiding you and Annie throughout your days and nights. I know some days are harder to get through than others. You and Annie are both doing really well. Annie is going to get a new job soon which will be much better for her and less pressure. She will meet new people. One person she met before will come back in her life and will reignite that twinkle in Annie's eye. Annie will be there for him like she was for me. He is a lovely, gentle person and you will get on with him too. Their friendship will be very special and everlasting.

Now that George is in heaven I speak to him differently. He converses and understands me from the spirit world. Dogs have a sixth sense. We are very intuitive and very psychic. George speaks to me, spirit to dog. When I am lying down, sometimes asleep making funny noises, I talk to George. It may sound to you humans that I talk in my sleep, twitching or dreaming, and maybe I am. However, I know what I am doing. Mother knows too. She doesn't interrupt our conversation. She knows he is near. Mother has her own way of speaking to George.

George taught me that in death there is freedom and new life. George isn't dead. George lives on in the memories of all the people he touched, sharing his love, helping and supporting everyone to go forward and get on with their daily lives. Like air, even though we do not see George physically, Mother and I feel and know he is around.

Saving me once again, he provides stability and strength like I have never known before. Teaching me to look death squarely in the eye, acknowledging its reality; telling me to be happy and smile again. Although I have been adrift in the dark sea of grief, the visit from George has brought me what I needed; a light to bring me great consolation and love.

George and I are together in a different way. A deep sensation of peace fills me. The burden of guilt weighing me down suddenly lifts, allowing me to break free and fly like a kite in the wind. It appears death isn't the end of life. Life still goes on. We are always loved and helped, being watched over by our dearly departed. Death is never an ending. Death is a new beginning.

'Teida, I'm finished pruning the lemon tree and am going inside. You want to come inside too?'

I follow Mother inside the house, and we both make our way down the hallway to a room Mother has been busily rearranging and reorganizing. We both sit together on the floor.

This room is where Mother has her collection of books, stacked high and low on the shelves of the bookcases. There is a large table displaying ornaments, candles and memorabilia that Mother and George both shared together. Across the back window is a large lounge with an oriental pattern of a red and black dragon. Cushions are placed on the lounge. Mother plays her ambient meditation music in the background.

Grabbing a pen and her journal, Mother starts writing. She writes and writes. All her thoughts come spilling out of her head. How do I know? Well, she tells me, and of course I keep watch over her. George tells me too. Curling up into a ball by the doorway, or on a blanket in the hall, I leave Mother deep in her thoughts and I drift off to another place, another world.

The phone rings and Mother answers.

'Hi Dad, how are you? Look outside, Dad, can you see any pink? The sun is setting and looks beautiful. Look out west Dad.'

'Did you end up getting the jumble word out today Dad?'

I come towards Mother, wanting to participate in the conversation.

'Dad, Teida says hello. She was a great help as I did a lot of gardening today Dad.'

'Teida, Dad says hello and gives you a pat.' Mother starts patting the top of my head.

As she hangs up the telephone, I nudge her, wanting to play ball. 'Teida, where's the ball? Go get the ball!' Mother says, encouraging me to get one.

Prancing up the hallway, I choose the orange roped ball and bring it to Mother, who is crouching down waiting in anticipation. Like a lawn bowl, she rolls it in a straight line, way down the hallway. *Where did it go?*

'Teida, go into the dining room, the ball is over near the table. Can you see it?' Galloping down the hallway, the ball catches the corner of my eye as I see it, at the wooden table in the dining area. *Oh, there it is. Why didn't I see the ball further away like I used to?*

—*Mother I found the ball. Here it is.* Plonk! I drop the ball in front of her. Mother rolls the ball again down the hallway.

—*I'm tired now Mother. Can we play later?*

'Teida, I can see you have had enough. We have had a big day, haven't we? You were a great help to me in the garden today. Time to go and get a drink of water.'

CHAPTER 22

THERE IS NO PLACE LIKE HOME

Another Christmas has come and gone. The days seem to be passing quickly. More than half the year has passed and Christmas is nearly upon us again.

'Morning Teida, time to wake up now.'

That's Mother's voice. Is it morning already?

We both walk out into the backyard. Mother sits on the garden bench while I go and sniff the lawn. With the clouds separating, allowing light to enter, I know that the sunrise isn't too far away.

After about ten minutes, we go back inside. Mother puts on the television for some background noise, then wanders out the front to pick up the daily newspaper.

'I'll get you some breakfast in a minute Teida. I don't have to rush today,' as she flicks through the newspaper.

Isn't today a work day?

Before long, Mother fills up my food bowl so I can have some breakfast. 'There you go Teida. You can have some breakfast now. I'm going inside to get dressed.'

She comes out wearing a t-shirt, blue pants and sandshoes. Those aren't her work clothes.

Each day that passes by, Mother dresses in her casual clothes. She flicks through the local newspaper, spends time on the computer and makes phone call after phone call.

Some days she stays home and other times she goes out.

'It is going to be a hot day today Teida, make sure you drink lots of water and stay cool. I'm going out for a while. I'll be back later.'

While I am passing time waiting for Mother to come home, a sudden gust of wind blows the side gate open. This gate is usually closed so tight Mother struggles to open it herself. The wind becomes stronger and stronger, whistling in my ears.

Looking left and right, I see the coast is clear. *Do I stay or go?*

I feel so lonely. Mother and I seem to be together more yet it appears we are in two separate worlds. Something seems to be separating us. I wonder if, now that George has passed away, I am a burden to Mother. Perhaps she would be better off without me. Perhaps going for a small stroll before Mother comes home would do me the world of good.

Walking through the familiar sticks, twigs, mulch and fallen leaves in the front garden I come to our driveway. In front of me is the black, smooth road. I take a stroll down the street, following the double white lines as the road curves in one direction then another, passing many houses left and right before coming to the end of the street, where there are no houses at all. Looking around I see a supermarket on the corner. Standing in front of the supermarket I stop and peer inside the glass. The doors suddenly open and someone walks out, carrying bags of groceries. I notice other people inside the supermarket. *Is one of them Mother?* The large glass doors open then close again.

Other people walk through the automatic doors, but not Mother, so I wander off.

I'm hungry. In front of me I notice something stuck to the concrete footpath. I have a sniff, then walk away.

To my right I notice some smaller shops. The smells emanating from these shops tingle my nose. A bakery with freshly made bread and cakes, a butcher with an assortment of meat displayed in the window, and the smell of hot food coming from a takeaway shop. All these odours would tantalize any dog. I hold my breath for a minute, inhaling all these new aromas. As I walk further, dirt and debris get stuck between my paws. I look at the traffic ahead, observing the cars, trucks and motorcycles all moving at considerable speeds, and I wonder when it would be safe to cross to the other side.

A deafening noise comes from my left.

What was that? I start running, too startled to worry about the traffic.

'What's a dog doing here, crossing the road?' someone says.

'Where's the owner?'

'Why isn't the dog on a leash?'

Gee, that was a huge truck. As I dodge the truck, another vehicle approaches not too far away.

The sound of a train passes by in the background. I look up. So that's where Mother used to catch the train.

Finally, I make it to the other side. Thoughts come flashing back to what George said as he came to say his final goodbye. *Make sure you look after Mother.*

I come to a sudden stop and look around. All the streets become a blur. They are now unfamiliar. *How do I get home? Will I ever see Mother again? George, if you can hear me, can you help me?*

Pedestrians are passing me left, right and center. Not looking where they are going, someone with a shopping trolley nearly bumps into me. I continue along the footpath for what seems to be an eternity, one step after another. Then suddenly a shadow captures the corner of my eye. I hear footsteps coming closer.

'Come here,' a gentle voice starts saying.

That's not Mother. I scamper away.

The same voice catches up with me. 'I am not going to hurt you. My name is Tim. I want to find your owner and get you home. I can see you have strayed away from your home and are lost.'

I run even faster and come to a large park that reminds me of a park I went to as a pup with Linda, surrounded by fields of grass here, there and everywhere. So much peace and quiet compared to the busy shopping center where I was just moments earlier. In the distance there is a children's playground, empty except for the odd person taking a stroll as a short cut through to the other side.

Taking a breath I hear another voice. This time the voice sounds as if it is coming from within.

—*Teida, it is George here. I understand why you wanted to run away. Now it is time to go home. Allow Tim to help you, he will get you home safely. I sent him so you can reunite with Mother.*

—*I didn't mean to George. I'm sorry. Will Mother be upset with me? Does she know I am gone?*

—*I know you didn't mean to. Mother won't be upset with you. She needs you Teida and you need her too. It won't be long Teida and you will be home again.*

Listening to George, I stop. Tim, a young man with light red hair, bends over and takes a look at my neck. 'I need to see if there are any contact details on your collar.'

Using his mobile phone, Tim dials a number. 'Hello, do you own a dog?' he asks. 'Yes, she is right here. I'll wait. We are at the cricket pitch in the local park behind the swimming pool. She is fine. I saw her while I was at the deli down town. She was dodging in and out of traffic and nearly got hit by a truck.'

Was Tim talking to Mother? I hope so. I'm scared. I want to go home.

I see a big white car pull up nearby. It looks like Mother's car.

'Teida! Hello Teida. What happened, where have you been?' Mother runs towards me with tears of relief on her face. Kneeling down, she gives me a great big hug and puts my leash on so we can walk straight back to the car.

'And you must be Tim. Thank you, thank you so much. Her name is Teida. The side gate blew open in the squally winds. The latch was down and the padlock was on. However, with the strong winds somehow the gate blew open. Teida must have been afraid of the winds and escaped.'

Mother pauses before continuing.

'Here, I want you to have this to say thank you.' As I look up, I see Mother giving Tim a box of chocolates.

'Come on Teida, let's get in the car.' We drive home.

'Teida, I am so sorry. I thought I pushed the latch right down and locked the gate. I came home. I called your name. There was no answer. I went to our neighbour across the road and then as I came home the telephone rang. I'm so glad Tim found you and I was able to come and get you. I would not know what to do if I lost you and never saw you again Teida. I love you so much.'

—*Mother, I am sorry too. I know you need me and I need you too. I didn't mean to escape and cause you any trouble. I love you too.*

The telephone rings.

'Hello Dad, she is home,' Mother says with total relief in her voice. 'The side gate needs to be fixed. The latch would not go down over the padlock. I am now going to keep Teida inside when I go out.' She ends the telephone conversation and starts talking to me.

'Here Teida, you must be thirsty,' Mother says, filling up my bowl. 'Teida I feel so alone, I am unsure what to do. I have been down in the dumps, not wanting to talk to anyone. All I want is George. I miss him so much. I realize that you understand me and I understand you. I forgot that. I am so sorry for what I have put you through. For twelve months now, I have had no work and not much money and no matter what job I apply for hardly anyone responds with a yes or a no. We hardly have any visitors, do we? It is just you and me. I am so thankful you are here. I would not know where I would be or what I would do without you.'

'I'm going out to check the letterbox Teida. I am waiting for some mail.'

Mother comes in the front door and I see her face beam with excitement.

'Look Teida, the letter I have been waiting for is here. I finally have a job, working as a community care worker. It is something totally different to being in an office doing administration and working at a computer. After twelve months someone has finally given me an opportunity to work again. I have to make a quick telephone call and let them know that I will be attending the upcoming information session.'

Mother dials the telephone number.

'Yes, I am available to attend the information session. Thank you so much for the opportunity.'

Listening to Mother on the telephone, I learn that she will be driving to different homes to assist the elderly with their housework. So different to the office work she used to do. George was right! Mother has new employment, a new career and less pressure. Now she is working closer to home and finishing work much earlier in the day than she used to, we end up spending most afternoons together.

CHAPTER 23

THE EXTRA PLATE

One thing that does concern me greatly is that Mother doesn't have anyone special in her life who is just for her. Since George's passing, Mother has a feeling of not belonging anywhere and not fitting in. There are the occasions when Mother tries to socialize, but some days I notice Mother straining to get through the day. George did tell me earlier that there is someone new coming into Mother's life. I wonder when that will be.

Mother swaps around the small glass rectangular table in the dining room and the tall large round table against the side wall of the lounge room. The two blue padded chairs next to the sideboard are put at the opposite ends of the round table, facing each other.

An extra plate, knife and fork is placed on the table, with white dinner plates placed in between. I can see Mother's drinking glasses standing tall. Incense is burning in the background.

—*Mother, what are you doing rearranging the furniture? You normally have dinner sitting on the lounge watching television. No one ever comes over for dinner.*

'Does that look right?' Mother mutters to herself. 'What else do I need to do?' She paces up and down before looking at the clock. 'I have no idea what I'm doing. Is there anything else I need to do? I only have half an hour before he arrives!'

—*Who are you referring to by 'he' Mother? Who is the extra plate for?*

'Teida, a man called Alexander is coming over for dinner tonight. You will like him. I haven't had anyone over for dinner for such a long time. George was the last person that has ever come over for dinner.'

Hmmm! I wonder if Alexander is that special person George told me about?

Pungent garlic combined with the smell of chicken wafts through the house as Mother busies herself in the kitchen. Did you know that one food that is really bad for dogs is garlic? Garlic can cause all sorts of problems in a dog's tummy. Although Mother's cooking is really flavorsome and yummy to eat, Alexander will just have to have my share.

—*Mother, I can hear someone's coming to the door. I think it is Alexander. I wonder what he looks like. Will he like me as well?* Walking to the front door I wait patiently and start wagging my tail.

There is a knock at the door, and Mother comes out of the kitchen to greet Alexander. I peer upwards.

—*So you must be Alexander. Mother told me you were coming over for dinner tonight. Hello, I am Teida.*

'Hello Alexander, come in. How was your day?'

'Really busy, but good. I have lots of proofreading to do. Sorry I'm late. After getting off the train, I popped into the supermarket to buy some groceries.'

Changing the subject, Alexander continues. 'Your cooking smells great! I've brought some drinks and dessert.'

'Thank you, I've just been making some garlic chicken and salad. Do you want me to help you with some of your proofreading?'

'Oh, would you? Thank you.'

'Alexander, I want you to meet my dog Teida.' I approach Alexander inquisitively, sniffing all around his feet. There is that same familiar smell from when Mother used to travel by train to and from work all that time ago.'

—Alexander I like your funky shoes and colorful socks. Do you know that Mother used to get the train home from work too?

Squatting down to my level Alexander gives me a pat. 'Hello Teida, I've been told a lot about you. I'm glad to finally be able meet you. You are very gentle, aren't you?' Alexander is similar in height to Mother. He has short brown hair, large, strong hands, and wears glasses. His sparkling green eyes light up the room.

I try to give Alexander a lick under his chin and miss.

—He is really genuine Mother, very friendly and I love his smile. I trust him. The last time I had a connection to one of Mother's friends in this same way was George. Intuitively I believe Alexander and Mother will have an everlasting friendship. I can see there is a very special connection between the two of them already.

I drop a ball in front of Alexander, curious to see his reaction.

'Sure Teida, I'll have a game of ball with you.' Alexander rolls the ball down the hallway, and I gallop down the other end to get it and roll it back to Alexander.

'You were quick Teida. You like playing ball. Are you ready? Here you go.'

'Are you ready for dinner Alexander?' Mother asks.

'Teida is a great dog. Did you know that dogs can show 200 emotions through their ears?' Alexander tells Mother.

—*Alexander knows that! I wonder what other facts he knows about us dogs.*

'She likes you too Alexander. Teida likes playing ball with people she has a connection with.'

Mother and Alexander sit at the table and eat. Then they have a bowl of ice cream each for dessert.

—*Alexander, how did you know that Mother loves ice cream too*?

Mother and Alexander start talking and I notice how much they are enjoying each other's company. The conversation flows then pauses then starts again. With his deep, articulate voice, even I can clearly understand what Alexander is saying. There is no tension in the air. They talk about gardening, music, and writing.

Sitting in the background, I listen as Mother and Alexander speak about a new topic called anthropology, which is the study of human beings, their origins, and culture. Anthropology is a big word for a dog like me. *I wonder if they know how a dog evolved from being in the wild to being part of human life?* After speaking about anthropology, Alexander and Mother start talking about the brain and music. *I like music. Music is good for the soul. Mother plays a lot of music. Does Alexander like the same type of music as Mother?*

Alexander is very intelligent. He has gained so much knowledge in his young life, seeing the world, learning about other cultures and then writing articles about all he has learnt and experienced. I see Mother can keep up with these new topics of conversation. She is at ease and comfortable, so much more relaxed than I expected her to be.

I wonder if Mother and Alexander want to know a dog's perspective. Even though I am lying down to rest, I listen and can understand every word they are saying.

Taking the plates over to the sink, Alexander helps Mother clean the dishes and the they rearrange the furniture, putting everything back in its original spot. Alexander puts the kettle on, making himself at home.

'Where are the coffee mugs kept?' he asks.

'In this cupboard Alexander,' Mother responds, showing Alexander the cupboard she is referring to. 'Just help yourself.'

Pouring the boiling water into the cups, Alexander and Mother have a cup of tea together. Mother shows Alexander around the house with me in tow.

'I like your atlas bookends and your dragon lamp. You have lots of books too – we can swap and share.'

Alexander collects his belongings, ready to go.

'Do you want me to drive you home?' Mother asks.

'That's very kind of you. Thank you.' He turns to me. 'Goodbye Teida, nice to meet you. I will come and play some more games of ball with you again soon.'

'Teida I am going to give Alexander a lift home. I won't be long.'

I love knowing that Alexander has come into Mother's life. Alexander and Mother have a really special platonic friendship. They have so much in common, and I like him too. He is so upfront and honest. Since that initial dinner, Alexander comes over frequently and gives me lots of pats and cuddles. I am pleased that Mother is able to help Alexander and he can be there for her as well. Besides Mother's family occasionally visiting, there hasn't been much human interaction in our home since George's passing.

Bit by bit, Mother starts smiling, laughing, and being happy again. Her inner soul is being filled up; it is not empty anymore. Her inner child is reappearing and she is having fun. Mother feels useful again, sharing herself with someone else and being part of another person's life. She hasn't done that for such a long time. Mother visits Alexander more frequently, sharing her knowledge of gardening and just sharing his home with him. It is so good to see her go out and about. Alexander will never replace George, but I am so delighted that someone else has come into Mother's life who loves and cares about her, enjoying her companionship just like George did.

CHAPTER 24

A RUN OR
A WALK?

'Hey Teida, do you want to go for an early morning run? Alexander wants to get fit and wants someone to run with him. I can walk, but I am no good at running. You are a better candidate than I am. You can run with the wind and Alexander will be able to keep up with you too.'

'Teida, with Alexander being interstate for a while, I have just sent him an email suggesting you be his runner. I think it is funny. Let me read it to you.'

Alexander, I found someone to run with you, her credentials are: she is female, very keen, has brown hair, very good looking, very active and runs fast like the wind. It is someone you know … guess who!

Mother rewords the next part to sound as if I am writing to Alexander.

Alexander, Mother said you want someone to run with … I love the outdoors and love running and would be good company for you. What do you think? The only thing is that you need to keep me on a leash and if you keep running forward I will be fully focused. Of course, I need the occasional drinking stop.

Alexander returns from his travels interstate. 'Hey, your email suggesting Teida being my running partner is a great idea. So we can all go together, how about we go on early morning walks?'

'When do you want to start – are you free tomorrow morning? Then if you need to you can come back and use the computer to work on your articles.'

'Tomorrow, yes let's go tomorrow.'

The next day, bright and early, Alexander comes over. Mother attaches me to my leash and off we go. With my tendency to pull strongly on the leash, it has been a while since Mother has taken me out for a walk. Outside, feeling the crisp morning air on my fur, I set off at a fast pace with Mother and Alexander having to hustle to keep up.

We walk up the street, passing the houses I see through the fence palings from my backyard, before coming to the main road. The traffic is traveling back and forth in both directions. Turning left I see silhouettes and shadow shapes from the sunlight bouncing off the trees and, with it being autumn, many leaves have fallen and are now crunching beneath my feet. On the nature strip at the edge of the gutter are large and small garbage bins waiting to be emptied, some with red lids and others with green or yellow lids.

From way up in the morning skies, the birds give a welcome, squawking or cooing their hello.

—*What was that?* I jolt with astonishment as an unfamiliar sound grabs my attention.

168

'That's just a truck passing by, Teida, nothing to worry about,' Mother reassures me.

Our walk turns into a brisk trot before Mother pulls me back. 'Not so fast, Teida. We need to wait for the cars to pass so we can cross the road.'

I notice these roads are black and rough, unlike the road at home where there are two white stripes painted in the middle and the surface is much smoother to walk on. As we walk towards the middle of the road, Mother, Alexander and I step up onto a round island in the center before stepping down so we can get to the other side. I notice cars of all shapes and sizes driving round and round in circles before straightening and driving off, one behind the other.

After crossing the road, we walk down a long street with many twists and turns as the path rambles one way and then the other. Many people are out and about, perhaps on their way to work. Some are in their cars. Others are riding motorcycles and some are standing at the bus stop by the side of the road.

'Here Alexander, you have a go and walk Teida. You can walk faster if you like.'

Alexander takes my leash and I surge forward as he extends the leash in front of him. He walks faster so there is no chance of me diverting my attention except to the smells straight ahead. I can tell by the way Alexander is holding the leash that he needs to relax more. He seems tense and appears to be under lots of pressure. Does he have lots of work to do or is there more that is bothering him? I believe Alexander has a lot on his mind, as if the weight of the world is on his shoulders. On our walk Alexander and Mother talk and talk, jumping from one topic to the next, admiring the surrounding scenery. They talk about their work lives, their families and just general chit chat.

We come to a pathway and, instead of being dry, the footpath has been splashed with water, wetting my paws. Looking down, I notice water trickling down the driveway. Someone must be watering their garden.

The concrete footpath disappears soon after and is replaced with soft earth and a rich green lawn. The blades of grass soak my paws with dew, so I decide to stand up higher, on my tippy toes. Alexander directs me onto the quiet road ahead. 'Teida doesn't seem to like walking on the wet grass.'

We pass so many houses, going up and down unfamiliar streets. Suddenly a pack of dogs come out from a front door and start charging towards their front gate. They begin yelping and growling. One gives a dominant bark and the rest join in. I know how they feel having a foreign dog walk past their home. In a dog's mind our job is to protect our home, and as part of our nature, we are very territorial. I feel like saying hello and introducing myself, but with Mother and Alexander leading the way I know it is inappropriate. Calmly, we walk straight past, without a care in the world.

'Good girl Teida, you did not bark at all,' Mother says. Directing her conversation to Alexander she comments, 'I counted five dogs in that house.'

We travel further up the street, and after a break in the traffic we cross the road and head back the other way. We arrive home. My leash is removed. Mother turns on the gas heater and goes off to work. Alexander stays behind to use Mother's computer to do some work. 'Teida, I need to finish writing an article and complete a grant application. I am really grateful to be able to use your Mother's computer. I really feel at home here.'

Emptying his backpack, Alexander spreads papers all over the floor. I have to be careful not to tread on them, so I find a spot behind the black chair at the computer and settle there. Kneeling down I notice Alexander's eyes wandering around, drifting from one place to the next. He looks in his bag and then at a pile of papers sitting on the floor, then back to his bag again. 'Where is it?' he says, exasperated. 'Don't tell me I've left the document at home.'

—*Which paper are you looking for, perhaps I can help you find it?*

'Found it.' He pulls out a page and I sense relief in his voice. 'Now I can start editing my article and complete my application.'

I look up at him and see Alexander's frowning face; his eyes seem closer together and he nervously puts his fingers in his mouth. Alexander stands and walks over to the computer. He seems so anxious.

Poor Alexander, he has lots to do. There must be something that I as a dog can do to help him.

Alexander leans back in his chair, getting himself comfortable. 'I have so much to do I don't know where to start. I almost forgot I have to attend a meeting as well.'

—*Meeting? What meeting? Is someone coming over here?*

Tapping his fingers on the keyboard Alexander gets straight to work, his eyes fixated on the monitor. I settle myself, curling up in a ball behind him.

—*Careful when you move your chair, Alexander, I am right behind you.*

171

Alexander slowly reads aloud a piece of his writing. One sentence after the next. Then he stops.

—*That sounds very good Alexander. You are really clever to write that.*

'No, that doesn't sound right,' he mutters to himself. He reads it again. It sounds slightly different to what he first read out. 'That sounds much better,' I hear him say.

Just as Alexander finishes reading his document, I hear another voice. Not Alexander's voice. It sounds like someone is speaking in an Asian accent. But with Mother still at work, there is no one else here besides Alexander and me. Looking up, I see Alexander talking. His voice is much louder and more articulate than when I heard it earlier this morning. Alexander's words are much more pronounced and he is speaking much more slowly. He pauses. *I didn't know computers can talk. Mother never converses with a computer.*

Another voice joins in, speaking in a different accent; they sound like an actor on television. 'Hello Alexander,' I hear them say. *Where did that come from?* With pen in his hand, and paper rustling, Alexander's attention is directed to writing. His hand is moving fast to ensure he scribbles down every word. He then stops and looks back at the computer, asking questions and expressing many ideas and thoughts about an upcoming medical research project. The conversation ends. As the voices disappear into the background, Alexander continues writing for a minute, then I see his fingers tapping away on the computer.

Alexander stretches before reaching for a book behind him on the floor. 'Oh, hello Teida, you have been really quiet sitting here haven't you?'

Before Alexander has a chance to open the first page of his book, his telephone rings. My ears perk up as Alexander answers his mobile phone in an abrupt tone. He rises from his chair and walks outside into the backyard. I follow close behind. Alexander paces up and down the lawn from one side of the yard to the other. He calms down a bit, then his voice becomes louder. 'Look I need to go now … I still have lots of work to do. I can't talk right now. No, I'll speak later … I don't know how long I'll be. Look, I'll call you when I'm finished.' He shrugs his shoulders and sighs. I feel his tension, his restlessness and his feeling of being under pressure.

—*Are you okay Alexander?* I give him a nudge.

'Thanks Teida,' he says, bending down to give me a pat. 'I am just feeling overwhelmed. There is so much to do. I didn't need that interruption. That call could have waited till after I was home.'

—*Yeah I know, phone calls can be a bother. Don't worry Alexander, you will finish everything. Mother will be home soon. She'll help you.*

Alexander walks inside and sits back down. 'Now, where was I up to?'

With Alexander back in focus on his work, I fall asleep. I am woken up by someone bashing on the side gate.

—*Alexander, Mother's home. She is at the side gate.*

Alexander rises from his chair and opens the side gate to let Mother inside. 'Hi Alexander, how has today been?' Mother asks Alexander.

'Getting a bit done, although not as much as I would like. I spent three hours on Skype speaking to work colleagues overseas about that medical research project I was telling you about. I thought it would only be an hour. Then immediately afterwards, my phone rang, and it took me so long before I could get back into the swing of things. There is so much to do and many deadlines to meet,' Alexander replies.

'You haven't had lunch, have you? Neither have I.' Mother says, stepping forward. Alexander rises from his chair. 'How about I put some curry pasties in the oven for lunch? You stay here and keep working. I will let you know when they are ready.'

'Thanks.'

After a while, Alexander wanders outside into the warm sunshine and heads straight towards the bench underneath the back deck. He lies down, his feet at one end of the bench and his head at the other. Alexander closes his eyes to have a doze. He seems so tired and stressed out. I am not sure if he is coping too well after that earlier phone call. Something really seems to be bothering him. I wonder if Mother knows.

Instead of staying by his side, I decide to go for a wander on the grass, thinking about what I can do to help Alexander. I stumble and fall, making a lot of noise.

—*Mother! Where are you? Alexander, can you help me?*

'Teida, are you all right?' I hear Alexander ask me. I see large shadows and hear footsteps coming closer. Looking ahead, I notice Mother and Alexander nearby. I must have had one of those fits again. At least this time I am out in the open on the soft green grass.

'Alexander, Teida just had a fit,' Mother explains. 'She will be okay. There isn't much you can do. Let's sit down and have some lunch.'

I get up gingerly on my feet and walk around, getting my bearings.

Mother sits opposite Alexander on the table at the back deck and they have some lunch together. I lie nearby, noticing how much they are at ease with each other and how Alexander seems to be a lot calmer now. Mother and Alexander really enjoy each other's company.

After finishing their lunch, I follow Alexander inside and he goes straight back to work. This time, Mother follows. She sits by his side and reads the article Alexander has just finished writing. Knowing that Alexander is in good hands, I lie down behind them and have a good rest.

'How is the grant application going?' Mother asks Alexander.

'Very slow and tedious. Are you able to read this section for me and see if it makes sense?'

'Is that word spelt correctly?' I hear Mother say as she points to the computer screen. A minute later she comments, 'The sentence in the second paragraph is it meant to read this paper or these papers.'

'Whoops! Thanks,' Alexander responds. 'Do you mind if I use your printer to print this page? I need to send it in the post today.'

'Of course you can. Give me the address of where you need to send it and I will write it on the envelope. How about I take a walk up to the post box and mail it for you? It will be better for you to concentrate on what you are up to instead of being distracted. Teida is with you. You sit here and continue working on the computer. I won't be long.'

With Mother gone Alexander, starts talking to himself.

'Now I need to finishing writing the article about being normal. How many words do I need to eliminate to stay within the word limit? Ten, isn't it? I can do that.'

—*Alexander, what is your definition of normal? Do you think I am normal?*

Mother returns from the post office. 'All done,' she says. 'Do you feel like a cup of tea?' she asks.

'Yes please.'

'Honey?'

'That would be great.'

Mother busies herself in the kitchen for a while before returning. 'Here is your tea Alexander, and some biscuits for afternoon tea.'

Alexander's voice lifts. He sounds much more cheerful than earlier this morning.

With the back door left ajar, I go for a wander outside and see the children playing in the street. *Can I join in?*

'Teida! Teida!' That's Mother. *Where is she?* I follow her voice and walk back inside.

'Hello sweetie,' Alexander says, bending over to give me a pat. He starts packing his bags.

'Thank you so much for helping me today Annie. I have been struggling a bit and would not have been able to accomplish everything if it wasn't for you. And thank you Teida for hanging out with me. I am glad you are feeling better now.'

Watching Mother and Alexander working together, sifting through papers and dockets, brainstorming ideas, suggestions and offering words of encouragement, I notice how much they really enjoy supporting and helping each other. Not a bad word is spoken between them. It brings back memories of how Mother used to assist George with his paperwork. I remember how Mother read George his correspondence and then George dictated to Mother a response to type up for him. With George being so sick, his eyesight was deteriorating so much that Mother became his second set of eyes. Things are similar between Mother and Alexander. Alexander writes and asks Mother to proofread his documents. She is Alexander's second set of eyes; finding any errors, amending documents where she sees fit and providing feedback to him. Alexander even helps Mother with her writing too.

CHAPTER 25

GROWING OLD GRACEFULLY

Now I am in my senior years; more gray subtly creeps onto my muzzle each day. I have arthritis trying to weaken the joints in my knees and legs, making them ache particularly on those extreme sudden changes of weather. The summer heatwaves or cold wintery days cause me to walk differently. I go and have checkups more regularly too.

'Yes that is the arthritis,' the vet explains to Mother. 'The arthritis is causing nerve damage in Teida's back. Teida will walk differently now. See how her legs are crossing in the front and how Teida is walking on tippy toes, with her right back leg scraping against the ground? This is all normal for a dog her age.'

Besides my arthritis, my weight is reduced – good for those dogs wanting to lose weight, but not me. I still eat the same amount of food as before. With the vet's advice, instead of once a day, Mother feeds me morning and afternoon.

'The loss of weight is expected for a dog her age,' the vet tells Mother. 'It is due to the muscle loss as a result of Teida's arthritis.'

The vet lifts me onto the table. 'No, you can't get off yet,' she says. Mother gives me a big hug, not letting go, while the vet takes a long stethoscope and listens to my heart. 'Her heart is good.' The vet looks at my eyes next. 'If Teida were a human she'd need to wear glasses. The cloudiness over her eyes causes her lens to harden, which results in a form of night blindness.'

So that's why I haven't been able to see so well at night time. I wonder if the vet realizes that I understand every word she is saying?

'Something I notice is that Teida stares at walls or into space. Sometimes it takes her longer to go to the toilet. She squats and then stops, looking at me as if to say, "Mother what do I do next?" Then her ritual starts again. Sometimes it can take her up to half an hour or more to go to the toilet. She has a tendency to forget what to do. Is that dementia?'

'Yes, dogs can get dementia just like humans. Teida probably does have dementia, and there isn't much we can do. I can see you take very good care of her. You are doing all you can.'

'Come on Teida, time to go home,' Mother says as she puts me safely in the car. Before long, we arrive back, and I am let outside into the backyard.

'Teida, how about a bone? You were so good at the vet's today.'

Yum, I haven't had a bone for a while now.

I sit in contentment, thinking about the various conversations between the vet and Mother. So, all my symptoms are normal for a dog my age.

I wander around the grass, sniffing for more bones. Did I eat it already? I wish there were more bones to gnaw. My tummy seems to have other ideas. Grumbling and growling noises seem to be coming from way down in my belly. *Don't tell me I am reacting to the bone Mother just gave me?*

I munch on the grass. I know that has helped me before. Then I feel total relief as my tummy empties from the inside out, all over the grass. I know now that bones cannot be part of my diet anymore.

Mother comes out. 'Teida, bones are no good for you anymore. You enjoy them so much but your tummy reacts badly now.'

Age definitely does take its toll doesn't it? There are good days and bad days; good minutes and bad minutes. Sometimes I trot next to Mother without a care in the world, and then the next time, stop! A senior moment.

—*Mother, where are you? I can't find you.* Walking along the hallway, I turn right and wander straight into the bathroom.

'Hi Teida, what are you doing here? You never enter this room. I wasn't too far away. I just brought the red bin inside from out in the street. Here I am.'

Puffing and panting, I get up and follow Mother as she walks from the bathroom to the living room and then to the kitchen. Short, quick, shallow breaths, one after the other. I feel exhausted.

'Teida, what's up? It isn't too hot today. Have you had a drink of water this morning? Come on girl, let me take you to have a drink. You haven't had a drink, have you?'

—*I forgot about the water. You are right Mother; I am thirsty. Thanks Mother.* Slurp! Slurp! *That's much better.*

Unsure what to do next, becoming totally immobilized, I stop as still as a statue and wait for her next move.

'Sit here Teida; I am just in the kitchen getting you some breakfast.'

—*Breakfast, yum! I'm starving! I haven't eaten anything since yesterday afternoon.* I wonder what Mother is making for me. I hope it is doggie muesli. Mother makes the best dog muesli. She mixes my medication with a sprinkle of sardines, a handful of oats and some of my dry kibble, and then drizzles it with some flax seed oil before mixing it through to combine all the flavors. Sometimes instead of sardines, Mother stirs through a smearing of plain yoghurt or a sprinkle of boiled rice. At the same time, she makes herself breakfast and we eat together. I usually wait until Mother sits and has her breakfast.

'Okay Teida, off you go, time to eat.'

—*Thanks Mother.* I eat my breakfast like there is no tomorrow.

'Not so fast Teida. You must slow down when you are eating.'

I finish my breakfast and go and settle on my mat in between the two lounges, not wanting to move. After a while, I hear Mother's voice again.

'Come on Teida, up you get, we need to go outside so you can go to the toilet.' Turning my head to one side, I look up.

—*Mother do I have to?'*

'I know you are settled snug and warm here, but I am going out for a while.' She takes a long look at me. 'All right Teida, I'll leave you here.'

The telephone rings. My paw cannot reach the receiver to say hello. Then it stops. Maybe they will leave a message for Mother to call back. I wonder who it could be.

Mother comes home a couple of hours later.

Passing by the telephone, Mother picks up the receiver. 'Someone has left me a message Teida.'

—*I hope it is Alexander, Mother. You haven't heard from him for a while.*

'Teida, Alexander called, he is coming over later today.'

Alexander's coming over. That's awesome. I can't wait to see him. I do miss those early morning walks we used to have together and those moments at the computer when Mother was at work.

Changing topic, Mother continues. 'Here Teida, I brought you a present, something to help you with those arthritic legs of yours.'

I watch Mother in anticipation as she unwraps the plastic and I see a large, round, woolly bed that she plugs into a power point nearby.

'Teida, I bought you a heated bed. A lady at the shop said it helped her older dog, so I thought that it might help you too.'

Walking to the heated bed, I discover I cannot see Mother when she goes into the kitchen. It didn't bother me before, but now I need her near me. I move and sit on the woolly mat in front of George's lounge.

—*There you are Mother. I can see you from here.*

Now I know how George felt with his sore hips and leg pain.

CHAPTER 26

REMEMBERING GOOD TIMES

Playing ball with George and the other children who came to visit was fun, but being much older these days, it wears me out. I remember all the fun times George and I used to have playing ball together and how it would put a smile on his face every time we saw each other. Let me tell you some of my favourite memories.

One of my favourite times was when I played hide-and-seek with the pink ball George gave me for Christmas. It was so much fun. George's face was priceless when I retrieved the ball from underneath the house after he and Mother tried to look for it beforehand, wanting to play with my new Christmas toy but unable to find it.

George was so kind. Every Christmas he always found me a strong tennis ball. Not just the normal size tennis balls but medium or large size ones in bright, happy colors. There were even balls made of rope intertwined together, combining colored strands of orange and white or purple and white. But of course my favourite is the last one he gave me, the bright pink ball that I still have today.

Another time that brings a smile to my face is when George came over to visit for the first time after losing his leg. I remember the expression on George's face when I walked over to his favourite lounge and he saw me sit on the floor in front of his chair and not move. It's a funny memory.

Spending so much time checking in on me when Mother was at work, George really helped me adapt to Annie's home during those first few months. No matter what we did, there was so much enjoyment on George's face.

Mother always gave me the freedom to create my own games, whether it be with the ball or just making everyone smile. I was able to show off my skills as a goal-keeper, dribbling and jumping up in the air to catch the large basketball before it went straight past me.

It wasn't just playing ball in the yard. I had indoor ball games too, where a ball would be rolled down the hallway and sometimes veered left or right. I even went into Mother's bedroom to fetch my ball amongst her shoes all lined up against her dressing table.

My arthritic legs are so sore these days, but I have been able to play ball without running too much. Instead of rolling the ball up and down the house, a ball is hidden in between my bedding and mattress, so I dig all my covers away to retrieve it. I stand right next to my bedding and see the shape of the ball looking like a big bump. Then I hear the words 'Go Teida, here's the ball,' and see Mother's arm pointing to where the ball is. I dig and flick the blankets all over the place. The ball rolls towards me while at the same time my bedding gets all tangled up in between my feet, finally uncovering the ball. Then after seeing the ball, I grab the ball in my mouth.

—*Found it!*

All these ailments never stopped me from running around and wanting to play. Even now I still have bursts of energy, although much briefer than before.

Mother wanders down to the spare room where she selects a book from her collection and starts to read. I follow, trotting behind with a ball in my mouth.

—*Here Mother, do you want to play ball?*

'Good idea Teida, we haven't played for a while. Will your legs be able to? Let's give it a try.'

—*Yes Mother, my legs are fine today,* I say as I drop a green roped ball in front of her.

'Are you ready? Here Teida, go and get the ball,' Mother says as she kneels down and crawls towards me.

Prancing down the hallway I go to get the ball.

—*Ouch! My legs hurt. Mother, I can't get up.* Slowly picking up the ball, I stop before walking slowly back to lie down.

—*That's enough Mother.* I collapse in a heap on the floor in front of George's favourite lounge. *I can't do this anymore. I thought I could. I want to.*

Mother lies down next to me. As she looks into my eyes, she says, 'Teida, I know you are unable to do what you used to. Your legs are sore, aren't they, and you are tired. You don't have to play ball anymore today.' She caresses me behind the ears and then gives my legs a gentle rub. 'You like me doing that, don't you?'

187

I turn onto my side, my back positioned as close to Mother's chest as possible. I fit perfectly between the top of her torso to the bottom of her knees, and she curves herself around me. I feel Mother's beating heart vibrating against my body, similar to when I was a pup and I snuggled up to my Mama, settling in for a mid-morning rest, pressing myself against her belly as she laid stretched out on her side. That was a while ago now.

—*Mother, can you rub my tummy?* I press myself further, right up to her chest, trying to get even closer and not wanting to move. Mother's hands rub slowly in a circular motion all over my tummy then her fingers massage me up and down, relaxing my body from my front legs to my back legs. I eventually fall asleep.

A few days pass by.

'Teida, from now on I am going to leave you inside while I go out. It is too hot and humid for you to be outside and, with your arthritis, if you stumble and fall you will be much safer inside being on one level compared to going outside and having to climb up and down the back steps. Here, I'll turn on the small square fan so it can keep you nice and cool.'

—*Thanks Mother. I am finding it hard to breathe more and more, and the back steps are becoming more difficult to walk up and down.*

I remember George didn't cope too well with those hot days either, particularly when he was sick and coming to the end of his life. With perspiration dripping from his face from the heat and humidity outside, George would spend more time hanging out with me under the cool air conditioner. It took so much out of him to inhale and exhale each breath. *Am I coming to the end of my life too?*

CHAPTER 27

ADVICE FROM AN OLD FRIEND

Mother closes the door behind her.

My blankets and sheets are now in the middle of the lounge room. Digging my paws into my bedding, I settle in for a mid-morning snooze. Rearranging my bedding is so exhausting, I don't know how Mother does it when she makes her bed every day.

Just as I close my eyes, I am woken by a shadow coming over me. I look up and see a familiar figure sitting on George's favourite blue lounge.

—*George, is that you?*

—*Hello Teida, how is my old girl?*

—*Hi George. I didn't think you were going to see me again after what I put you through by running away. Mother has been leaving me inside now when she goes out. The weather is so hot these days all I want to do is sleep. When it is cold my legs are so sore I stumble and fall. The falls are not like my seizures. I even* lose control of my bladder or bowel which is really embarrassing. Mother says these seizures are mini strokes. George, I want to be strong, but my legs feel so weak that I just can't move. My mind wants to be active, play ball and run around; then when I do my legs are so sore and it doesn't take long before I lose my breath. I puff so easily George. George, I remember breathless you became, how you found it hard to cope with those hot and cold days and how much pain you were in.

—I was never good coping in hot weather Teida, and becoming older makes you more sensitive to the change in temperature too. That is why Annie leaves you inside more. Inside is nice and flat, outside the ground is uneven, and there is a step or two. She knows you cannot cope with all you used to and doesn't want you to stumble and fall. Annie wants you to rest. She wants you to live your days in comfort.

I gasp for air before continuing.

—George, it isn't just the weather that is bothering me. The other day, George, it took me over 40 minutes to go to the toilet. Mother was so patient. Some days she hasn't got that much time when she has an early start at work. I know how to do it. Why does it take me so long? I start the normal routin,e then I stop and stare into space. I hear Mother's voice or she claps, and that puts me back into the rhythm again. When I last went to the vet they said that I may have doggie dementia. Is there such thing as doggie dementia George?

—Teida, growing old is a normal part of life. You are sixteen years old, a senior citizen now. Just like my body grew old and worn out, your body is doing the same thing. Those sore hips and knees of yours, feeling like they crunch as you walk, is your *body weakening. Even going to the toilet as you do, your mind is digressing, wanting to be in both the physical and spiritual world at the same time. Teida, being old means sometimes forgetfulness, for dogs as well as humans, and yes, dogs can get dementia too.*

Teida, do you remember how Annie was my eyes when I couldn't see? Well, now she is your eyes. Annie is the one you look up to when you are unsure. There will be days where you can play ball and other days where you need to rest. There will be days where you remember and days where you forget. There will be moments where you can control what to do and other times where you will have an accident. These are all symptoms of doggie dementia and mini strokes. Even though your life is coming to an end, you are going nowhere soon. You are not ready yet and neither is Annie. You will know when that time is near. Do what your body allows, Teida, and when you have those moments of forgetfulness Annie and I will always be here to guide you.

—George, did you see the new bed Mother brought me the other day? My bed is so comfy, so soft and fluffy with lots of padding. One side it is warm and woolly for the winter and the other side is cool for the summer. I like to stay snuggled up, wrapped in warmth, not wanting to move.

—Yes Teida, your new bed looks so warm. It is good for your arthritis.

—George, Mother will be upset when I go to heaven. She will be on her own. Living here alone. I worry about her George. She is so brave, has so much courage, yet that smile, that happy smile she had when you were here, well, I only see glimpses of that now George. She will need lots and lots of support when I am gone. But I am not really going anywhere yet, am I George? I am not

191

ready to die, not yet George, but when I do my soul will always remain in Mother's heart. Do you know when it will be my time to go to heaven?

—*Teida, your time is coming to an end. It will be soon, but not yet. Before it is time you will learn more about death and dying and so will Annie. Annie has a lot of inner strength Teida. She is strong and brave. There will be lots and lots of support for her to get her through. Life won't be the same for Annie when it is your time Teida, but be assured she will be looked after. Teida, something big will happen before it is time. You will need to support Annie more than ever. A big tragedy is coming, one that will change Annie so much that she won't be the same person that she used to be.*

—*A big tragedy? What is it George?*

The front door opens, interrupting my conversation with George. He floats upwards, watching from above.

'Hi Teida, I didn't expect to be out so long. Come on, let's go outside.'

Opening the back door, a gust of hot air hits me in the face. *I am so thankful Mother kept me inside today.*

Growing old is something new to me. After speaking to George, I now find being in my senior years much easier to deal with. These days, being much slower and more breathless, I am more content to enjoy the simple things in life; just snoozing and hanging around Mother.

CHAPTER 28

SADNESS IN THE HOUSE

In the depths of the night, a blaring loud noise startles me. The back door squeaks open and closed. 'Ouch! My foot!'

That's Mother's voice. It sounds like she is far away. Mother, what's wrong, where are you?

The loud noise stops just as fast as it started. The back door is pushed open. Mother tip toes quietly back inside. Noticing me at her feet, she pauses and looks around, then approaches the chair nearest to her.

I look up and sniff her feet.

—Mother what's wrong with your foot? It smells different. The odour tells me there is something terribly wrong. Mother's left foot seems to be double the size of her right foot and has tones of black, blue and even purple.

'Teida, I don't know what I've done, but I've hurt my foot badly. I went to turn off the alarm system and rolled my left foot going up the back step.'

I see Mother's anguish on her face as she attempts to put one foot in front of the other, hobbling a few steps to the fridge. After grabbing something cold out of the freezer she hops over to the lounge and plonks herself down, her foot elevated.

'Teida, I hope the ice-pack works tonight, otherwise I'll have to go to the medical center first thing in the morning.'

After a while, I hear pitter pats as Mother limps down the hallway to her bedroom.

Poor Mother, I hope she hasn't injured her foot too seriously.

The next morning Mother gingerly walks out into the living room. 'Teida, I'm going to the doctor. I can't put my foot down onto the ground. I can't walk. Look at it, my foot is twice the size of the other foot and is so black and blue.'

Finally, after what seems like an eternity, Mother arrives home with a strange, gray, heavy looking boot that seems to be hiding her foot and half her leg. The boot doesn't have a leathery smell like Mother's shoes. Actually, it has no odour at all.

'Teida, I've fractured my foot. I cannot return to work until the fracture heals. I am unable to wear shoes anymore.'

Mother pauses.

'Teida, I'm going up to Alexander's. He is at home while renovations are being done and has invited me up for lunch. I'll be back soon.'

Days and nights pass with Mother hobbling from one part of the house to the other. Mother cannot sit on the floor unless her foot is straight out in front of her, although she does kneel and give me cuddles and pats. She has to sleep with a pillow under her foot. Days and nights pass. Every little task now takes twice as long.

The phone rings.

'Teida, my mother is in hospital. She broke her hip and the social worker needs to see someone from the family before she can go home.'

Grandma-Mother hasn't been well for such a long time. Her health is deteriorating rapidly. I wonder why the social worker needs to see someone so quickly.

A few hours later Mother returns, her face despondent. 'My mother has shattered her hip Teida. I saw the social worker, who is trying to determine what she needs so she can go home. She cannot stand up anymore and may never walk again.'

The next day arrives.

Mother picks up the telephone. It's Grandma-Mother.

'Hi, how do you feel now you are back home? Do you want me to come down and help you?'

Mother hangs up and starts crying.

'My mother is upset Teida. She is so angry and I cannot blame her. I wish I knew what to do to help her.'

Being at home day and night, sitting by the phone, brings back memories of when George was seriously ill and dying. *Is Grandma-Mother dying too?*

With Mother traveling back and forth to see Grandma-Mother on a regular basis, I stay inside longer and longer. Some days when Mother comes home that day has turned into night. It takes me back to the time when Mother was working late, until dark, and visiting George when he was unwell in hospital. This time, though, I am kept inside – not left outside.

Mother and I fall asleep. Mother wakes up and hobbles to the living room. She turns on the television and switches it off again. I see an expression on Mother's face and sense that Grandma-Mother will go to heaven soon. Thinking back to the conversation with George, I now realize why I haven't crossed over to the spirit realm. This is the tragedy that I need to help Mother through.

Mother's birthday is in a week's time. Will Grandma-Mother last until Mother's birthday?

'Teida, I am having a few people over for my birthday on Sunday. Dad is going to come over. I am seeing my mother the day before, on Saturday. I hope she lasts till I see her, it may be my final visit.'

Saturday arrives. Mother drives to Grandma-Mother's. With Grandma-Mother being so sick, I believe that this is the last birthday they will spend together as mother and daughter.

Mother comes home later in the afternoon, loaded with goodies. 'Look Teida, look at the tea towels my mother gave me for my birthday.'

She holds the gift in her hand. 'I am not sure how long she has. She is now finding it difficult to talk and I gave her a notepad and pen so she can write all she wants to say. She hardly eats now and is tired all the time. My birthday is tomorrow, do you think she will get through the night?'

—*I hope so, Mother.*

In the morning, bright and early like an excited child, Mother bounds out into the living room. Today is her birthday. The telephone rings. There is an early knock at the door as Alexander quickly drops by. Just as Alexander is about to leave, Mother's happy face turns into anguish, with tears welling up in her eyes that she is trying to keep away. Stuttering, and looking down at her mobile phone, I hear Mother say, 'She may not make it through the day.' She shows Alexander.

Mother's family and friends arrive. I could see Mother is torn with different emotions deep inside. She is trying to be happy, yet deep down she is so uncertain, knowing each moment that passes may be Grandma-Mother's last breath.

After a few hours, Mother's guests go home. It is just Mother and me. 'Hello,' Mother says as she picks up the telephone.

'What! So how are you getting there? Are you staying the night? I'll let you know. I can't leave Teida inside if I stay overnight.'

I just heard my name. Where is Mother going? The phone rings again.

'Hello Alexander, it's Annie. I'm going to say goodbye, do you want to come? If I end up staying overnight can you drop by and let Teida out in the morning?'

'Teida, my mother may not make it through the night. I need to go and see her. Everyone in the family is going so we can say our final goodbyes. If I stay over tonight, Alexander will come by in the morning and let you out. I love you.' She kisses me on the forehead before letting herself out the front door.

I sit and ponder before eventually drifting off and waking up in pitch darkness. I hear the key turn in the lock.

—*Mother is that you?*

For the following few days, Mother continuously drives down, day after day, her fractured foot protected by her moonboot.

Today is Tuesday. For some reason today that feeling returns from all that time ago. The same gray empty feeling I felt when I saw George for the last time. Something tells me that today is the day that Grandma-Mother will be crossing over to heaven.

Mother talks on the telephone and quickly gets dressed before racing out the door.

All of a sudden the afternoon sun comes beaming inside the living room, casting shadows on the coffee table. The telephone rings once then stops. A light flickers on and off, then disappears. I realize what has just happened. I just know. Grandma-Mother has just passed away. She has now gone to heaven. I wonder how Mother is coping.

—*Come home safe Mother; I'll be all right.*

Night time arrives. Mother is finally home. She looks at me, stunned and lost. Her mind has been put into automatic and she is shocked, unsure what to do next. She kneels down and holds onto me. I stay by her side and wipe the tears flowing down from her face. This is the tragedy George warned me about earlier.

Alexander calls by on his way home from work with some takeaway dinner for Mother. He goes home.

A week passes. Today is Grandma-Mother's goodbye service. Another extra long day inside, or so I thought.

The clock strikes three. The front door opens. Who is there?

—*Hello Alexander. Boy, I'm glad it's you. Open the back door quick. Where's Mother, is she with you?*

Alexander unlocks the squeaky back door and immediately I race outside. He places some items on the back deck table one by one. *So that's where the tree lopper was.* Together, we both come inside.

It reminds me of the times when George used to come by when Mother was at work. It is great to have some company when Mother is out.

Climbing onto the dining chair, Alexander stretches upwards and changes the light bulb in the dining room. He sits down and writes a couple of notes on small, yellow pieces of paper before walking out the front door and closing it behind him.

—*Goodbye Alexander, I'll see you soon.*

People come and go, similar to when George passed away. Stillness, darkness, exhaustion and despair as one day turned into the next. When George passed away years earlier, it taught me so much about humans and how they deal with life and death. These days Mother seems so alone, so despondent. Not being as active as she usually is, because of her fractured foot, doesn't help. *Will Mother ever be able to walk again*? Eight weeks later, it seems that her foot will never heal.

Today, Mother has another doctor's appointment. After what seems like an eternity, finally she comes home. Standing on the either side of Mother I am greeted by two long, metal-looking sticks. I step back. Hopping from one end of the house to the other, I can see that Mother can no longer put her foot on the ground. She looks so unbalanced and cautious. She appears more fragile as she manoeuvres herself around, in between each piece of furniture, in and out of each room, trying to dodge me in the process. In place of the moon boot, I can see Mother's toes peeping out of a white fibreglass cast.

'Teida, I saw a different doctor today. He said the moon boot was no good and that if I'd had a fibreglass cast and crutches in the first place, my foot would have healed. The reason it hasn't healed is because I have been putting my weight on it to get around.'

Poor Mother, now she is really immobile. How will she get around? How will she feed me and even clean up after me? She can't carry anything anymore.

One week after the next passes by. Winter turns to spring. Mother kneels down, shuffling from one room to the next before climbing up onto the chair in the kitchen.

—*Mother, do you have any lunch for me?*

After eating her lunch, Mother gets down on her hands and knees and makes her way to the spare room. Then she comes out with the vacuum cleaner in her hand and starts vacuuming the house one room at a time.

'Teida the floor is so dirty, it needs a vacuum. It hasn't been vacuumed for such a long time.'

—*Be careful Mother.*

Finally, she sits on the lounge and elevates her feet. I fall asleep nearby.

Waking up I hear Mother moving around in pitch darkness. She must have gone to bed before wandering out to the living room and now she is sitting on the floor at the coffee table in front of her computer. Stretching upwards, she turns on the blue lamp and heater behind her. The clock chimes twice. She starts writing in her journal, pouring out all her emotions and feelings. The flame of the radiator heats up the room. After a while, Mother curls up on the floor, the heater still on behind her. She must have fallen asleep.

Winter turns to spring. Even though there are more phone calls to check how she is, not many people visit or offer to lend a helping hand. Flitting in and out, people pop in for a short time. Grandpa-Dad and Aunty Sam help when they can, yet I see Mother's struggle.

'Teida, all I want is company. I know I have you, but I just want a hug, someone human to pop over and say hello and just be there. Everyone is so involved in their own lives. Why aren't people more proactive? You know, people reached out when my mother injured herself, yet it is totally different with me, and what makes it worse is that I miss my mother. I miss her terribly. I am so glad you are here. I couldn't handle it if you left too. People I thought I could depend on, I can't, and those who do come over flit in and out. I am not good on my own dealing with grief; I need a shoulder to cry on, and no one is here.'

Mother starts crying.

'I am here for anyone and everyone, whenever they need me, and when *I* need someone people are just too busy. Instead, I have to manage by myself. It isn't fair. Why can't people go out of their way to give me a helping hand around the house, make a cup of tea or just keep me company? I know people work and have family lives, but what about a quick phone call or an SMS to just check and see how I am managing? I am no good going up and down stairs and even walking down the street to get a loaf of bread is too far with a fractured foot in a moon boot. I normally heal quickly, and my foot is taking such a long time. It is now over four months. I don't know how long it will be before I can walk again.'

Poor Mother. She will get better. I know that. Things are hard for her now, but she is strong. Walking on her knees, she goes from the living room down the hallway and back again, giving her arms a rest from those steel crutches of hers.

Eventually, Mother does walk again. It was more than six months before she was able to put a shoe on and return to work.

A DIFFICULT CONVERSATION

It is coming up to my seventeenth birthday, and I just feel so exhausted these days, even more than before. I rest and fall into a deep sleep that takes me to another place. I am not in this world but transported somewhere else, into another time, another place. Then I am pulled back and, waking up, realize that perhaps it was just a dream. It takes me a while to work out that I am lying on my mat. I know that Mother is not far away. Soon after I stare into space and fall asleep again. Today though, I feel more energetic. I stand up and go exploring, wandering clockwise around the living room through to the kitchen and back to the living room again. Everything seems unfamiliar, yet I know it isn't. I walk in circles for a few minutes or more before tiring myself out for the rest of the day.

There seems to be such a big difference in the temperature outside to inside that I now feel uncomfortable sitting outside on the grass, enjoying the mid-morning sun. Mother decides to give me a brush and I pull away. More and more hair comes off me with each pat, with each stroke of Mother's gentle hand caressing me. It's strange though because I really enjoyed having Mother brush me. Now everything seems to take so much longer and take so much effort that I puff and pant. I seem to take faster and deeper breaths. I really need to talk to Mother about something important; not a pleasant subject but one we all face, both animals and humans.

'Teida, I know you are coming to the end of your life. I want to make sure you are comfortable. I want to do the right thing by you. I want to understand you more. I want to prepare you and me as much as I can. I contacted an animal communicator who will talk to you and then tell me what you have to say, or I may ask questions, and you cam answer them. She sounds lovely.'

—*Mother, you have lifted the weight off my shoulders. There is so much I want to tell you and I wondered how to communicate dog to human.*

Sitting and staring at the computer, like Alexander did previously, Mother speaks to a gentle and caring lady. Her voice is so clear that I can hear it from the computer as well. Listening, writing and talking, the three of us are all in a conversation together.

'Annie, Teida wants to talk about death and dying. Are you okay with that? Then we will answer any other questions you may have.'

'I had questions about this subject too. If it is a priority for Teida, then it is a priority for me.'

—*Mother I have to tell you, my life is coming to an end. It will be as the new growth comes on the trees, and before the hot weather.*

'Dogs talk in seasons Annie, and not time. Teida is telling me her time will end in spring.'

'Teida will be seventeen on 6 September. Will it be before or after her birthday?'

'Teida will reach her seventeenth birthday. That means she is almost 120 in human years. She looks good for her age but is very frail and old, Annie. It won't be long after that. Dogs do not know time like humans. There is no today or tomorrow, and even 24 hours is a long time.'

—*Mother, my body is causing me great discomfort. I cannot settle anymore except on my nice warm bed in the corner or my blankets in front of the blue lounge or in the hallway. As my frail body becomes less and less functional, I just find it hard to do what I used to. My organs are slowly shutting down. I can't quite settle and rest easily.*

When I am out the back, there are too many distractions, many sounds I used to enjoy hearing I find disturbing, like a car driving down the street. The birds chirping are high pitched. I am more sensitive to the temperature outside, whether the sun is warm or the wind is cold.

The animal communicator, looking at Mother's face, speaks to me. 'Teida, your mother doesn't want you to go. She is scared but knows she wants to do the right thing by you. You both are so connected to each other.'

There are so many things to say, aren't there? This isn't as hard as I thought.

—*Mother, I know things will be difficult for you when I am gone, but I will never be gone. I will always be right beside you.*

'Please never leave me Teida. I know your time to go to heaven is soon, and you will be up there with George, my mother and your puppy family. Just promise that you will be with me and when it is my turn you will be there to greet me too. I wish I could come with you, but I know it isn't my turn yet.'

Mother takes a deep breath and diverts the conversation to the animal communicator. 'So what can I do for Teida to help her through her last days? What vet?'

—*Mother, I prefer the young man. He is compassionate and gentle. Not the older man, he doesn't have good energy.*

'Teida would prefer the young male vet to the older one.'

'Teida has never been to the older vet. He just passes through in the waiting room. She had surgery on her mouth and her feet, and it was the young vet who did that.'

'The young male vet is the one she wants. She wants you to feel comfortable calling him and asking him to your home. You will need to invite the vet into your home Annie, and you need to feel comfortable with that.'

'So will Teida be put down?'

'I can't say for sure, but you need to be prepared either way.'

—*So what does that mean? What happens when I get put down?*

The lady explains what happens when the vet comes over.

—*Teida, I sense you find it difficult to let go and leave Annie. When it is time, you may need help with that. What happens is you will have a vet come over to your home to help your transition over to the other side. You will know when Teida. Annie won't be strong enough to take you to the vet, so the vet will come to you. He may give you one or two needles. One needle is a pre-med which helps calm you down, and another with a green substance is to put you to sleep in a way that you will never wake up again. The second needle is very fast acting Teida. You will snore and then stop breathing. There is no pain. You will go to heaven and be at peace.*

The lady then talks to Mother. 'I just explained to Teida the process of being put down. Her mind is much more at ease now.'

—*Mother I would rather you put me to sleep than die naturally. I am finding it a struggle, but I am not ready yet.*

The lady continues where I left off.

'Teida is telling me she wants you to make the decision instead of letting her die in discomfort. Annie that is a gift from you to Teida. You have the feeling already of when it may be. Her physical body is breaking down, and she is finding it difficult to get around these days.'

'Annie, when the vet comes over to help euthanize Teida, you need to make sure you spend time with Teida alone. Do you know whether you will bury Teida or have her cremated?'

'I do. I am going to have her cremated so then she is with me everywhere I go.'

'So before the vet takes her body away to be cremated, make sure that you spend one on one time with Teida alone. Wrap her in one of her warm blankets and stay with her for a while. Have a support network around you. Prepare people now so they are with you when you need them to be.'

'Teida do you have a particular blanket you want me to wrap you in?'

—*The one I lie on Mother. I like that one.*

'Anything else Teida, do you want me to do anything else?

Do you want me to scatter some of your ashes in the garden? What type of service do you want?'

—*Whatever you want Mother.*

'Teida doesn't mind Annie, as she won't be in her physical body anymore. Honour the day and do things to support you. A service is a human thing. She doesn't mind what you do. Animals understand death and are not concerned about what is done with their physical body. One thing they do, though, is they leave part of their soul with their owner. So Teida will leave part of her soul with you so you will know she is around you.'

Changing the subject, the animal communicator continues. 'Grief is the thing that is most misunderstood, Annie. There is no time limit for grieving. Take all the time you need. You have a special connection to Teida. She loves you and you love her. Everyone grieves differently. It may take a long time. You have a deeper connection with Teida than people realize. You need to grieve and be surrounded by family and friends who have no problem with you grieving.'

The lady uses a very gentle voice as she talks to Mother. 'Putting Teida down will be the biggest decision you will ever make, but at the same time, the best decision for Teida. You will give Teida the most beautiful gift of letting her go into the spirit realm and not making her hang on when she needs to go.'

'What happens if I am at work and it is time?'

—*Mother, I'll wait for you.*

'Teida can wait until you come home or up to the weekend, as long as it isn't months or weeks.'

'No, I won't do that to her.'

'I know you wouldn't,' said the animal communicator. 'Teida

will sleep more and more. Let her sleep. She is not incontinent. One day she will be good, and another day she may not have the energy to eat her food.'

'She is sleeping a lot already. Can I wake her up to go to the toilet?'

'Of course you can. You are waking her up as you are doing the right thing by Teida. Also, her mind will start to slow down. It is the normal process of dying.'

—*Make sure you have a good support network Mother. Alexander, Aunty Sam, Grandpa-Dad, anyone who makes you feel comfortable and who will be there for you. I know it will be hard. I will find it hard to leave you too Mother. When it is time Mother, I want to be at home, like Grandma-Mother was, no vets, no hospitals, just home with you beside me. And Mother, don't worry, I'll tell you when it is time. You will know. Going to the vet is too much for me now.*

'What about seeing people for the last time?' Mother asks.

—*Mother, don't worry. Before I go, I will end up saying goodbye to all those I need to. I understand Alexander is busy, but if possible, one main person I really would like to see is Alexander.*

The animal communicator gives Mother some words of reassurance. 'Annie, don't worry, everything will fall into place. Teida will see all those people and even Alexander before she crosses over. Everything that is meant to be will happen.'

I saw weight lift off Mother's face. In a shaky voice, she continues talking, asking every question possible.

'Is Teida in any pain at the moment? She had trouble with her ears recently, and I think they are still bothering her.'

'Antibiotics do not work anymore for Teida, Annie. She has had sore ears for quite some time.'

'I've taken her to the vet and they haven't picked anything up.'

'It is deep within Teida's ears – particularly her right one. They need a good clean out. They are not painful, just uncomfortable, that's all. I'll send you some Australian Bushflower Essence to help Teida's ears. Teida doesn't want to go to the vet anymore. Teida wants to be at home now.'

'And what about Teida's tummy? It grumbles and she sometimes smells as if she has wind, but I know she hasn't.'

'When people get old, Annie, they have a certain smell to say that they are an old person as their body is breaking down. Teida is a very old dog and her body is breaking down. So that is a normal process for Teida. Also, as animals get older, their skin becomes thinner – like humans – so Teida is unable to stay warm like she used to. The blood comes closer to the surface, which makes her colder. She will follow you around a lot more too.'

'She does that already. She puts her head in my bedroom to make sure I am there. She wanders up and down the house to find out where I am if I am not close by.'

'In the end, she may even sleep closer to you. Teida is not just anybody. You are a part of her and she is a part of you. You are family. I see you both are soulmates. You are a sensitive being Annie. You need to surround yourself with people you feel comfortable with and who understand you. It will be a struggle so make sure you have company and get all the support you need.

'Is Teida okay with me being upset? If I get angry with someone on the phone Teida runs away as if I am yelling at her.'

'Teida is fine. Being upset doesn't worry her. What worries her more is when you pretend that you are not upset and sad and you are. Teida notices your energy changes when things upset you. It is in her own best interest that she steps away. Dogs are more sensitive. They are like sponges and they can absorb things on a deeper level. Mind you, no human is completely open to everyone either.'

'Teida likes to snuggle up to me and have her back touch my heart.'

'Your energy is beautiful and nurturing for Teida; she likes feeling your heart against her.'

'What about getting another dog?'

'At this stage Teida says there are no plans for you to have another dog. When it is time, she will guide you. Animals choose us. Just relax and if it is meant to happen, then it will happen. Do what you feel is right for you Annie. Just be open to whatever comes along.'

After about an hour after our conversation with the animal communicator, Mother turns to me and gives me a big hug.

'Teida, I know you are old and your time here on earth is coming to an end. I keep thinking of last summer and how hot it was and I wonder how you are going survive this summer, being even older and more frail. I look into your eyes and know that time will be soon when you will go. I know I will feel sad so I am thankful that I can stay home and spend more time with you beforehand. My main concern is then what? I will be here on my own and that scares me.'

I see in Mother's eyes how lonely she really is. Mother really needs a special person to support her through her grief and loss.

I couldn't bear to see her suffer like she did when George passed away. Grandma-Mother died recently, and people came and went, but only for a short while before going back into their lives again. Despite Mother being there for her family and friends in their times of need, at the moment, it seems Mother has taken a back seat in many people's lives and is not everyone's priority anymore. Grandpa-Dad and Aunty Sam keep in touch regularly. I hardly see Alexander these days, although he does flutter in and out every now and then. He must be busy. I miss him.

I hope someone special does come into Mother's life. Will I meet that special someone who will keep her company and share her thoughts? I believe I have already met that person. Only time will tell. I know I told Mother to get another dog when it is right for her, I hope she does. She really needs company and is so good with animals. I never thought we would get on so well when I first came here and now we are the best of friends. I know another dog will not replace me. Like humans, dogs are unique in our appearance and personalities.

When it is my time to go, I know George will be there to meet me with open arms and both of us will watch over Mother, and Grandma-Mother will be watching too. I believe that if Mother was to go before me, I would fret badly and wouldn't leave my home, being always by her side. I know that whenever the time comes, I am ready for God to take me by the paw and lead me to the other side.

I try not to think about what it would be like if Mother went first and I was left here on my own. I now know it will be the other way around. How will Mother cope without me? Who will be there to look after her?

ALMOST BUT NOT YET

The clock chimes once on the hour. It must be one in the morning.

—*Mother! Wake up, I need you!'* I make my way up and down the hallway, catching my breath more with each step I take. *Mother.*

'Teida, what's wrong? Teida, I'm here. Hang on puppy! I'm coming.' Her deep and groggy voice tells me she must have been in a deep dream.

—*Mother, I need to go outside. I have a sore tummy.*

Staggering from her bed, Mother feels on the wall for the light and switches it on before finally unlatching the back door. That all too familiar lurching, retching sound erupts inside of me. I race around the yard before stopping.

—*That feels much better.*

'Teida are you all right now? That is unlike you, wanting to go in the middle of the night.'

After waking up the next day, that same uncomfortable, queasy feeling returns. *Oh no, not again!*

The cool breeze brushes past my face as I make it to the back deck. There I see Mother with my brush and I walk away.

Mother follows for a while and sits on the floor, holding onto my collar with one hand and with her other hand she starts to remove the build up of moulting hair on my back and particularly in between my tail. I walk away.

It seems an eternity before I notice Mother waiting patiently for me to return and together we make our way inside. Mother stands at the kitchen bench and I watch. 'Teida, come and sit here.'

These signs tell me that it isn't long now. Almost time to leave the earthly world, my Mother and all those before me. I look into Mother's eyes and realize she knows too.

I hear Mother talking. No one is around.

'George, I know Teida is dying. Her time is coming to an end. Promise me one thing George: please look after Teida. Can you and Teida please watch over me? I wish I could come with you. I wish Teida and I could go together. I know it isn't my turn yet. I'll be all on my own now George. How do I go on? Can you help me?'

—*You need people around you now. Prepare your family and friends for what is coming up. While Teida is in a stable mind, give everyone the opportunity to say goodbye to her. Know though that even though you want certain people to see Teida beforehand, if they choose not to, it is their doing. Right now Annie, you need to honour your feelings and do what is best for you. Creating a tribute and having a small gathering would be lovely for Teida.*

After talking to George, I hear Mother's fingers tapping away at the computer. She stares at the screen.

'George, how does this sound?'

To my beautiful family and friends.

As most of you know, Teida is slowing down. She will be seventeen on Sunday and after that her time is limited. Her organs one by one are shutting down.

This week she has taken a turn for the worse. On Sunday night and last night, I was woken up by a panting dog and when I took her outside, she went to the toilet and even vomited once in the morning.

So what I am asking all of you is that if you want to spend time with Teida before it's too late – to just hang out, to say your goodbyes or both – please do it sooner rather than later as after Sunday I cannot guarantee how much longer she will be around … It may be days or weeks – I know it is not months.

Teida thinks the world of you all – your families, your spouses and those in your life. She has enjoyed hanging out with you all. She thanks you all for being a part of her life as you are mine. Yes, you can bring your children to have a pat (she cannot play ball anymore).

I also ask for everyone's support and patience to help me through. Teida is my best friend, has helped me through the most difficult times in my life, has been there when I grumble, or when I have something exciting to share, when I wake up at some ungodly hour in the morning when I need someone, and no one is around. Seeing my best friend go through her final days is hard. I try and be strong and positive, but with Teida leaving me I do have my ups and downs. There will be days where I feel lost and alone and just need some company, whether it be a hug, someone to talk to, someone to say they understand. I am no good on my own dealing with grief and even now, after 70 days, I still and always will miss Mother. I understand everyone has their own lives to lead and have other priorities – children, work, family, social activities, etc. So, when you say that you are too busy, please just send a quick email, an SMS, a Facebook message or even a phone call to check how I am doing.

When it is time, there will be a gathering of family and friends. I hope you can come. It will be one day in the afternoon to account for those who are overseas and want to be a part of this gathering, yes, I can use Skype, and anyone else who is away for work or a short break please let me know so we can organize a suitable time for everyone to be there.

Perfect!

Each day comes one at a time. Sleeping becomes my regular pastime. I listen as Mother opens the front door, but instead of checking who it is, I stay curled up, snuggled, not bothering to move.

I'm suddenly woken by the prod of Mother's foot touching me. Following Mother outside into the spring mid-morning sun, I feel the warm of the sunrays shining down, warming the ground below. I stroll up and down the yard, hearing the birds chirping their songs, feeling the sun come and go like the clouds that make their way across the sky.

What a glorious day to be outside! I burrow my head into the grass and take in the different smells before taking a wander down the side and having a look through the gaps in the back fence. I seem oblivious to what's around me as

I walk round and round in circles past Mother as she calls my name.

'Teida! It is getting hot, time to go inside now.'

'Teida! Come on girl; it's too hot out here.'

Totally exhausted, Mother and I make our way inside, I flop down and close my eyes. Realizing Mother isn't nearby, I wake up.

—*Mother, where are you?* I wander down the hallway, peeping my head in one room then the next. Then I hear rustling in the bedroom.

Putting my head around the bedroom door, I see Mother walking around one side of her bed before sliding on top and then pulling the sheets and blankets. She stops.

'Hello Teida, I'm making my bed. Come inside and have a look.'

I take a step back. Before I disappear, Mother kneels beside me and massages me behind my ears. We face each other and look into each other's eyes. Mother wraps her arms around me, clinging tightly.

—*Mother, I feel so weary these days. I am so tired.*

'I know Teida, you sleep much longer these days. Sleep as long as you need to. Resting and sleeping is the best thing for you at this time.'

Changing the subject, Mother continues.

'You haven't been in my bedroom before, what do you think?'

'Your bed is so high Mother. The carpet is so soft and woolly.'

'You know Teida, I'll miss you when you go. It won't be the same anymore. You're my best friend Teida. I love you. Thank you for being my best puppy friend in the whole world. I love you puppy girl.'

Mother's family and friends pop over one by one to see me.

'She has slowed down a lot.'

'Teida used to be gray around the muzzle; now she is white. She looks ancient now.'

'Teida looks very uncomfortable.'

'Teida is a lovely dog; it is a shame to see her go. Try not to think about it.'

'She is very unsettled.'

'Why are you hanging onto her? You need to let her go.'

'She couldn't find a better mother.'

'Hello Teida, did I wake you up? You are tired aren't you?'

'She looks good for her age.'

'Teida is active though,' someone remarks as I walk around and around in circles, becoming unsettled and uncomfortable.

My health picks up for a while. A couple of months pass. Today I get that funny dizzy feeling again and am unable to stand up. My fits have returned. Mother looks at me as she talks on the telephone. This fit seems to be over just as quickly as it started. I follow Mother around the house before settling in the corner on my mat with Mother next to me on the floor caressing me as we look into each other's eyes.

'Teida I see angels around you – small angels all in a circle above and the color orange.'

'I see them too Mother.'

'Your time is near now isn't it?'

'I'm afraid so Mother.'

I make my way to the other mat in front of the blue lounge.

Mother joins me on the floor, lying in front. She rolls me over so my back is against her beating heart. Today though, it isn't as easy to turn as the other days.

The tick of the clock tells me about half an hour has passed by. I stand on all fours and slowly make my way outside. And I mean slowly. One foot in front of the other, or in my case one paw in front of the other. Then it happens. I stagger, large big steps from one end of the lawn to the other. I want to go to the toilet, yet my legs shake. I stagger and stumble and just make it to squat before collapsing immediately afterwards, unable to move. I realize my fit was never over.

I hear Mother's feet running towards me then she drags me over to the other side of the clothes line – closer to the pathway nearing the back deck. I look in her eyes.

—*My fit is different this time Mother.* Finally, after what seems like 20 minutes or so, I stand up on all fours, puffing and panting with each breath.

By this time Mother's neighbour arrives. Staggering one step at a time I make it inside to the living room. I look down to my comfy bed in the corner. 'It's a long way down to my mat Mother.' She watches with anticipation as I eventually flop, exhausted by the whole ordeal, breathing rapidly one breath at a time.

'Here Teida, I've put your fan on for you.'

—*Thanks Mother, I am so hot. I am finding it so hard to breathe.*

Mother's family come over – her sister, Grandpa-Dad and her uncle. 'Where is she?' I hear one of them say.

'Here Teida, do you want to have a drink?' I see my water bowl in front of me and turn my head.

'She isn't good.'

'She is very weak.'

'She has lost a lot more weight since the last time I saw her.'

Meandering to the laundry, I take a sip of my water before making my way back to the lounge room. Time takes so long to get from one place to another now.

—*Mother where are you?*

I stand up and notice her in front of the freezer. 'Here Teida, have some ice block.' I look and walk away.

Eventually, after what seems like an eternity, I make my way to the laundry and have another drink before plonking back down on the floor, exhausted.

Everyone leaves one by one. Mother looks into my eyes. 'I know Teida.'

I know my time now, coming closer – really close. I still worry about Mother. Who will look after her, be there for her? She will need extra, extra support now.

CHAPTER 31

MOTHER'S FINAL WISH

Each day becomes hotter than the day before. Puffing and panting, slowly I make my way down the hallway, following Mother as she makes her way to her bedroom. I come to my sheets and woollen rug on the floor. It seems much warmer down here compared to where my fan is up the other end of the house, but despite the heat, I need to stay by Mother's side.

I hear Mother make her way towards me. She grabs me by the collar and I slide from the hallway across to the bathroom, feeling the cool tiles beneath me. With a cool, wet face cloth, Mother gently wipes me down from my face all the way to my tail. My breath changes from rapid to slow calm breaths before I rise to my feet and become stable enough to walk back to the living room.

Mother turns on the ceiling fans and my small square fan. The cool air blows in my face and all over my body, causing me to eventually drift off to sleep.

I hear the sound of the television, then silence. I look to my left and find Mother nestled on the lounge. I look again, unable to see her, and I go for a walk.

'Teida. Teida.'

—*Mother is that you? Where are you Mother?*

'Teida, I'm out here puppy girl. I'm on the lounge. It is too hot for you to sleep in the hallway.' Together we walk back to the living room and settle down for the night.

I wake myself up, gasping for air. A gentle hand caresses my head. Mother comes to the rescue. She goes to the freezer and I stand up. 'Teida, today was 38 and tomorrow will be extra hot, even hotter than today. They say it will be 41 degrees. Tonight is a warm night. Here is a midnight snack.' I hear something hard land on the kitchen floor and know Mother has thrown me some ice block.

Did I hear Mother say that it will be 41 degrees? It is only November. *How am I going to get through such a hot day?*

We both settle down again. What seems to be a short time later, I hear the clock chime four times. The cool air from the air conditioner in combination with the ceiling fans makes its way in my direction.

Mother rises and kneels in front of me before stretching out one leg at a time. Her soft, gentle hands slowly move up and down my back. We look into each other's eyes before I turn over and have her heart touch me. Mother leans over and kisses my forehead. I now realize how I will get through today, this very hot day.

Throughout the day Mother bites off more ice block and drops each piece on the floor in front of me – one at a time.

She rinses off my small green cloth underneath the tap. Placing it gently on the top of my head I find it as cold as the ice block, and know Mother put the cloth in the freezer. The air of my fan becomes more powerful as Mother turns the switch to a faster mode.

Throughout the day Mother continuously wipes me down with my cloth, gives me more and more ice blocks and, as I change where I am sitting, Mother follows me with the fan. She comes and sits by my side. 'Teida don't worry, I am going to make sure you survive this very hot day.'

Night time arrives, and finally a rush of air comes through the front door. I know that if Mother was at work today, I would not have made it. I know that with each breath I take my time isn't far away, my time to go to the spirit realm. I am ready, yet at the same time, I feel sad and worry, knowing how empty Mother will feel being on her own.

I look at Mother and notice relief in her face that I made through yesterday. Yet I see anguish and uncertainty. I sense her pain, her confusion and anxiety.

Mother puts her hand to her chest. I feel her grief and loss. She walks to the bathroom and leans over the bathtub. I hear a sound I haven't heard in a long time. Standing outside, I see Mother reach and turn on the tap over the bathtub before rising to her feet. She makes it out to the living room and collapses onto the lounge.

After a short while, the telephone rings. Mother starts crying. Crying like I have never heard her before. Crying out to the world, emptying her heart and soul, expressing the truth all built up inside her.

'I am not going to put Teida down,' I hear her say. 'Just because Teida is slower than she was yesterday is no reason to put her down. Yes, she needed help to survive the heat, but anyone elderly whether it be animal or human would need help. I find it hard to survive the heat at times too. Teida is mobile, she is eating and drinking, and if I put her down I am putting her down in human time, not in divine time. That is not right. I am not going to be forcing her to go down because that is ego. Teida will tell me when it is time. The day Teida is unable to stand up, the day she is unable to eat, drink or go to the toilet, that is different, but I am not going to force her to go before it is time. I am sick of people telling me that I need to do the right thing and it isn't fair that Teida suffers any more. She isn't in any pain or suffering. Do you think I would let her suffer and hang on if she is? If Teida was in pain, she would not let me touch her and would not follow me around the house. She wants to be near me as much as she can.' Mother sobs and sobs before finishing the phone call.

Mother kneels over me and hugs me, not wanting to let go. I feel her wet tears on my fur, similar to when George passed away all that time ago. Yet today was different; I feel a weight lift off Mother.

'Teida, I am not going to have you put down. I know in divine time you are going to the other side and I accept that. What I do not accept is for someone to come to put you to sleep early. Early before it is time, just because you are slower than yesterday. You want to be near me and I want to be near you. You may be in discomfort, but I can see you are not in pain; I see you are breathless, but I see other humans and animals breathless too still living. Your time is not now. It is when God wants to take you; it is when he is ready for you to go and my mother and George will be there to welcome you.'

Mother takes a breath. 'I am ready when Teida is ready. God, I know Teida's days are numbered. For my Christmas present, are you able to make Teida spend Christmas with me? I couldn't handle both Mother and Teida not being here for Christmas. I know it will be Teida's final Christmas. If Teida is in too much pain and suffering though and you need to take her earlier, I do understand.'

I look into Mother's eyes with sympathy and understanding.

—*Mother, I'm not ready yet. You will know when. Ignore those people. You and I are both going to spend Christmas together.*

Sitting down on the floor surrounded by Christmas wrapping, Mother cuts paper to size and individually wraps one item after another before placing them under the Christmas tree. She then writes Christmas cards, placing them on the table ready to be mailed. Then she stands up, switches off the light and goes off to sleep.

A streak of sunlight pokes through the blinds, creating shapes on the carpet before me. I slowly meander down the hall, looking for Mother, and I find her sitting on the floor in her reading room with only a dim light shining.

'Hello Teida girl, you were sleeping, I didn't want to disturb you. I am writing in my journal.'

Mother leans over and crawls towards me. I take a step backwards.

'No need to be afraid Teida, I want to give you a pat. You know I think you will make it till Christmas, there is only a few days to go.'

I stop and look into Mother's eyes. Mother kneels in front of me as I sprawl myself across the blue rug in the hallway.

—*Do you think I really will make it Mother?*

'Of course you will Teida, there is only two days to go now. Besides Santa has something very special for you.'

I lay down with Mother behind me and I fit my body against her chest. Just the two of us intertwined together on the floor. I feel the warmth of Mother against me.

Early the next morning I hear rustling as Mother tosses and turns beneath her bed covers.

Mother's awake, and it is totally dark.' The garbage truck passes by in pitch black darkness. The garden waste truck empties our green bin before driving by. I know it is this truck as it comes much earlier in the wee small hours of the morning. This morning it is extra early.

Mother rises from her bed and turns on the lamp. The Christmas tree sparkles with all its decorations and many presents from family and friends sitting underneath. 'Teida, you made it! Santa's come. Look, he left you a Christmas stocking with lots of new treats that you'll enjoy.'

'Thank you so much God. Thank you for allowing Teida to spend her final Christmas with me.'

I sit with Mother next to our Christmas tree. I see Mother's eyes half closed and half open. I know she hasn't slept much.

Like every other year, she starts waking up all her family, starting with a phone call to Grandpa-Dad and then Aunty Sam.

This Christmas, Mother is hosting Christmas lunch. Grandpa-Dad and Mother's uncle will be coming over for lunch. With Mother standing at the stove, wafts of roast turkey tickle my nose as she opens and closes the oven. It won't be long before Mother's guests will be coming over.

Against all the odds and with the miracle of God, the universe and those passed before us, Mother and I spent what we know will be our final Christmas together.

MY FINAL BREATH

Today is New Year's Eve. Mother starts to walk down the hallway in pitch darkness. *Is it that time already?* I felt like I had only just fallen asleep. We both go outside into the backyard. Today though, something feels different. My body isn't the same. How can I tell Mother I am not feeling good today? How can I tell her not to go to work today?

'Come on Teida, let's go outside.'

I start walking and suddenly feel myself bouncing up and down like a buoy in the ocean.

'Teida, come here, you seem to be walking differently today. No, that's not good. Can you make it up the step? Let's go inside. I don't want you falling over.'

Still with the same instability, I follow Mother, worsening with each step I take.

—*I'm sorry Mother, I can't walk like I used to anymore.*

'Teida I am not going to work today. I can't leave you this way. You are suffering aren't you?'

I don't know what I should do. I feel so sad for Mother.

'It's all right puppy girl. You sit here and rest. It's time isn't it?'

I look into Mother's eyes.

—*I didn't know how to tell you Mother, but I'm afraid so.*

Mother picks up the phone, making one call after the next. I see sadness as tears well up in her eyes. She sits down waiting, before pacing the floor.

'It's time isn't it?' I hear her say again.

Soon there is a knock at the door. 'Hello.'

I know that voice. It's Alexander.

'Let me get you a tea,' he says to Mother. Alexander looks in my direction then towards Mother. 'She isn't good on her feet is she?'

'Alexander, am I doing the right thing? I called the vet. He is coming around at lunchtime. The cremation people are coming soon after. You know I don't want to do the wrong thing by Teida.'

'Yes, she isn't stable anymore. You are very brave Annie. I am very proud of you.' They both embrace before sitting together and having a chat. Then Alexander kneels over, looks into my eyes and gives me a pat. We say a few words to each other before he leaves.

—*Alexander, please do me a favour – promise me that you will look after Mother.*

I stand up to follow Alexander to the door but only get as far as the coffee table. As much as I want to move further, my legs stop in their tracks, not wanting to. I can't go any further.

'Look Alexander, Teida is trying to stand and say goodbye to you,' Mother says with a brave tone in her voice.

They both look in my direction. Alexander gives me a wave, then leaves. Mother comes over and sits by my side. The tick of the clock sounds in the background. The phone rings, disturbing the silence, but not for long.

Mother and I go outside. It has been a few hours since I went outside and boy I need to go. It seems as if it has taken all my energy to get from the back door to the grass and now I have to walk all the way back inside again. Mother waits patiently at the back door.

The front door opens. Grandpa-Dad makes his way inside. Mother, sitting on the floor next to me, caresses me against her body. No words need to be said. There is the click of a camera or two as photos are taken of our final moments together.

Grandpa-Dad rises and I feel well enough to follow him around the house, bouncing up and down with each step. He seems so tired and frail today. He returns to the lounge room. Meanwhile, I continue roaming around, walking around and around in circles before pausing for a halfway break and then returning to where I started. I see Mother.

Oh there's my mat. 'Come and sit here Teida,' I hear Mother say as I puff and pant with each breath. Finally, I make it back onto my mat. Grandpa-Dad kneels right next to me, giving me a final pat before sitting on the chair next to me. I feel his comforting strength as he says his final goodbye.

—*Thank you for looking after me Grandpa-Dad.*

Someone was missing.

—*Where's Mother?* Instinctively I rise before realizing that Mother has turned around, walking towards me.

'Here Teida, look I have some lemonade ice block for you.'

My head turns in all directions. I follow Mother's scent, and as I come closer to her, the smell of lemonade ice block becomes stronger.

'Here, have some more.' Mother bites off some more and drops it on the floor nearby. Mother keeps giving me small bits of lemonade ice block until eventually it all disappears. 'That was good wasn't it girl? I'll get you some more.' Our moment is disturbed by a knock at the door.

Grandpa-Dad rises from his chair and goes to the front door. I follow to check things out and notice a familiar man with a suitcase – the young male vet I normally go to see.

I know why the vet is here. I walk around, passing the dining room, round to the kitchen and back again – round and round in circles once more. Eventually, I am gently guided back to my mat.

'Hello Teida,' this familiar voice says. 'Yes she doesn't look good and based on her age even if we did find something wrong like cancer, there isn't much we can do. You as her owner know her more than anyone else. Putting Teida to sleep is the best thing to do.'

'It is probably one of the not-so-pleasant things you do, isn't it?' Grandpa-Dad says.

'Well, it gives me an opportunity to say goodbye too. Teida has been a very good patient. She is a lovely dog. Things are worse when the owner keeps their pet alive when they are so unwell or when an animal dies unexpectedly, like on the operating table, from something other than what you are treating them for.'

'I'm sorry Teida,' Mother says, her eyes welling up, not wanting to cry. She holds onto me from behind with both hands tighter than ever before.

—*Mother you are doing the right thing. I couldn't go to heaven without you. You will be all right. Even though I am going to doggie heaven, I will never leave you. I will always remain in your heart and soul forever.*

'So how will the process work?' Grandpa-Dad asks the vet.

'Teida will only feel a small prick. The process will be quick. She will close her eyes like having an anaesthetic but not wake up anymore. Afterwards, she may empty her bowel or bladder or both, and perhaps have a small gasp of air, and that is all normal,' the vet explains.

I start shaking and then stop. Nothing. I feel Mother's body leaning against mine. There is total stillness and silence. I now float upwards and see Grandma-Mother, George, my dog Mama and Da all waiting for me. I feel so much lighter. I realize that I will soon be able to run around and play again. The arthritic pain in my hips and legs begins to disappear.

With the vet now gone I see Mother huddling over my physical body. She wraps me in my winter jacket and puts my Christmas goodies beside me. I see she wants to cry yet it seems she doesn't know how. The cremation man finally arrives. He and Grandpa-Dad wrap my body in one of my cotton sheets before carrying it to the van outside. The cremation man drives away.

Looking down I see Mother holding back her tears of despair, trying to be so brave, and Grandpa-Dad consoling Mother. They soon leave. Mother is now alone with her own thoughts. I brush past her as she walks from one end of the house to the other, wondering if she knows I am near. Sadness fills her heart. She looks around and sits on the floor, looking around her. Everything is so quiet. Mother sits with her journal and grabs a pen. She writes and all her thoughts come pouring out. She kneels and with a spiky brush in her hand brushes her carpet, sorting out the dust from my hair.

—*Mother, you can throw my fur in the garden.*

She walks out the back and quickly returns. 'I can't stay out here for too long, how do I manage without Teida?'

I see Mother jumping from one thing to the next. Mother returns to work and comes home to an empty house with no greeting at the door, so distraught and tired. Day turns into night. She falls asleep on her bed and wakes up in the middle of the night with no dog following her up and down the hallway.

—*Mother, why are you up so early? It is 2am.* Mother, oblivious to my thoughts, rearranges the furniture, setting the table with serviettes, plates and cups and serving platters. She gets the large coffee urn and coffee cups and arranges them neatly in a line on top of the sideboard. 'I'm going to give Teida a wake,' I hear her say. 'Animals deserve a send off just as much as people. Teida needs to have the best wake I can give her.'

—*A wake, isn't that just for humans?*

The day of the wake arrives. Chairs are spread out in rows. There are tissue boxes on the coffee table next to Mother's computer. The timber box with my cremated ashes is placed on the round table in between the blue lamp and the candelabra. I see many familiar faces, Mother's neighbours, Grandpa-dad, Aunty Sam and, of course, Alexander. They all sit on the lounge and the many chairs spread all around in the lounge room.

All of a sudden the computer starts talking and Mother answers back. The television is turned on with everyone, even the computer, facing the television, and I see myself as the starring attraction.

Everyone watches a tribute Mother has made of all the times we had together – playing ball and growing old. Then each of Mother's guests shares special memories, reflecting on the fun and most memorable moments that they all had with me. I never realized how much I touched everyone's lives.

To finish off, Mother shares with everyone a special piece of writing, a poem she wrote thanking me for being in her life. And Mother, I want to thank you too. You are the best person a dog could ever have. You are not just a dog owner; you are my best friend. I love you Mother. Even though I am now in spirit, I live within your heart, and I will always stay by your side guiding and supporting you each day forward eternally forever.

Teida

by Danielle Corrie

Thank you for sleeping in the hallway and being my shadow
Keeping me company when no one is around
and cheering me up when I am down.

Thank you for entrusting me with your life
and being my best friend
For being patient with me, accepting me
and taking care of me.

I miss seeing your excited face
Greet me as I come in the door
And as I go out you say 'do you have to go?'
And as I come in you say 'let me out, quick!'

Teida you've had your fits and stumbles
with the odd accident or two
But no matter what I wouldn't change a thing
And would do it all again.

Teida you've got me through good times and tough times
From when I was made redundant to my parents' divorce
And now more recently my fractured foot
You helped me when my best friend died
and not so long ago with my mother.

When there is no human contact to say
I'm here – are you okay?
You've looked into my eyes and said
I'm here, it will be okay.

Teida I love you and miss you
Life will never be the same without you.

Now that you are in heaven
Please promise me you will guide me
through each day
And stay by my side forever.

ABOUT THE AUTHOR

Danielle Corrie is a first-time author, community care worker and business owner. Throughout her whole life Danielle has always been surrounded by family pets big and small, from dogs to parrots, to an aviary of budgerigars and even a goat, a duck and a turtle who lived in the family home. As a result, Danielle became a lover of animals. In particular, Danielle has a personal affinity with dogs, who automatically connect to her gentle nature and temperament.

Through Danielle's work as a community care worker helping people to live independently in their own home, Danielle liaises with many people, both young and old, who have a variety of pets. These animals show Danielle how to read different animal's energy, improving her animal intuition skills. In addition many of these clients, like Danielle, have experienced the loss of a loved one and as a result, Danielle has developed a connection to the spirit world.

Besides her work and personal experience, Danielle's education includes palliative care, courses in preventing and understanding dementia and aged care. On a personal level Danielle has also studied Reiki as well as Indian Head Massage. Danielle has a great passion and interest in connecting to the other side. Her growth and experience has culminated by her being approached to participate in a pilot documentary about psychics, which was recently televized.

Danielle assists people with proofreading and essay writing and through much encouragement from a particular friend, who proved to Danielle that she is a writer, she has now written her first book.

First published in 2018 by New Holland Publishers
London • Sydney • Auckland

131-151 Great Titchfield Street, London WIW 5BB, United Kingdom
1/66 Gibbes Street, Chatswood, NSW 2067, Australia
5/39 Woodside Ave, Northcote, Auckland 0627, New Zealand

newhollandpublishers.com

ISBN 9781760790349

Group Managing Director: Fiona Schultz
Publisher: Alan Whiticker
Book Consultant: Rachel Yoog
Project Editor: Rebecca Sutherland
Designer: Sara Lindberg
Production Director: James Mills-Hicks
Printer: Toppan Leefung Printing Limited

10 9 8 7 6 5 4 3 2 1

Keep up with New Holland Publishers on Facebook
facebook.com/NewHollandPublishers